D0556470

Packing with Llamas

Fourth Edition

By

Stanlynn Daugherty

C LAY PRESS, INC.

Publications
Pioneer, California

Packing with Llamas by Stanlynn Daugherty

Published by Clay Press, Inc., P.O. Box 250, Jackson, CA 95642.
Printed in Canada.

Fourth Edition, first printing 1999

DISCLAIMER OF LIABILITY

Library of Congress Cataloging-in-Publication Data

Daugherty, Stanlynn
   Packing with Llamas

   Bibliography: p.
   Includes index.
   1. Backpacking - Oregon.   2. Llamas - Oregon.
I. Title.
GV199.42.07D38 1989   796.5'1   89-8048
ISBN   0-916289-18-4

What reviewers say about this book:

"A book the llama community has long been awaiting. Stanlynn Daugherty puts into the written word the feeling most llama lovers can't adequately express about human/llama bond that one day hits us and changes our lives forever ... The book is friendly, humorous and full of Ms. Daugherty's personal experiences."

Llama Life

"Compelling reading, an excellent reference ... Stanlynn Daugherty has definitely done her homework. *Packing with Llamas* is very complete. The eight appendices are worth the twenty dollar investment in and of themselves ... Once you begin this book, you are likely to be caught up in its flow. I was quite taken by Stanlynn's natural style and captivated by her stories."

Llamas: The International Camelid Journal

Contents

Stanlynn Daugherty

About the Author

Stanlynn Daugherty has been leading llamas into the wilderness since 1984. On her ranch in the Wallowa Valley of northeast Oregon she keeps a herd of more than thirty llamas, specializing in breeding and training pack llamas. As a commercial llama packer she has led trips for the Sierra Club, Elderhostel, Womantrek, the High Desert Museum and other groups, as well as guiding "Learn to Llama Pack" trips for prospective packers. Horse experience from the age of five including work on cattle ranches and packing mules as well as several years as a travel agent provided the background for her llama activities. She has served on the Packing Committee and Board of Directors of the International Llama Association and on the Board of Directors of the Eastern Oregon Outfitters and Guides Association. Stanlynn is a two-time recipient of the International Llama Association's Pushmi-Pullyu award for her work in disseminating information on llama packing, and has taught packing clinics across the United States, as well as in France and Switzerland.

Photo and illustration credits

The author took the photographs on the front and back covers as well as the photographs on pages ii, 2, 3, 7, 8, 16, 19, 21, 23, 29, 32, 35, 42, 46, 51, 55, 59, 62, 66, 71, 73, 87, 90, 93, 94, 107, 119, 123, 124, 103, 132, 134, 135, 136, 141, 145, 146, 149, 150, 153, 156, 157, 158, 161, 166, 172, 176, 191, 197, 201, 205, 207, 208, and 210

Other photographs were taken by Kelly Hart (6, 75, 101, 115, 137, 147), Rosana Hart (58, 194), Jan Marts (xiv), Marty McGee (viii), Gary Miller (48), Jeff Moore (97, 108), and Doris Woempner (49, 57, 67, 79, 88, 89, 99, 103, 104).

The drawing of the llama on page 25 is by Janet Hohmann, and is based on a drawing appearing in the November/December 1986 issue of *Llamas Magazine*, in conjunction with the "Form, Function, Conformation, and Soundness," by Murray E. Fowler, D.V.M. and is used with permission of Dr. Fowler and the magazine, as is the list in Appendix Three.

The other illustrations including the gravity water filter system, pack bag pattern, and rubber band connector were done by the author on a Macintosh computer.

Cover photo: Jay Rais and Dagwood at Slickrock Falls in the Eagle Cap Wilderness.

Foreword

By Ann Ronald

Like so many inveterate backpackers, I never considered llamas or even horses as hiking companions. On the trail, I believed in self-reliance - my own broad shoulders and my own two feet. I'm no longer young, though; my back aches under a heavy load and sometimes my arches hurt. The spirit may be willing, but the body objects.

Still, I never pictured llama-power until a visit two years ago to Hurricane Creek. There I met Stanlynn Daugherty and the offspring of Lydia and Annapurna. Coal-black except for a white fringe across his eyebrows, the week-old Alby bobbed and bounced back and forth from sunshine to shadow. Dcvi, an off-white female with a day's more maturity, peered cautiously around a tree. Together, dark and light, the two baby llamas would have captured the heart of any animal lover anywhere.

I watched them for hours, took countless rolls of photographs, then left for the nearby wilderness and ten solitary days of backpacking. When my blisters and I returned to civilization, Alby and Dcvi looked just as cute, but their older, packing counterparts in the next pasture looked downright endearing. That night, I dreamed of my gear fixed on their backs instead of mine, I heard the thud of cloven pads instead of lug soles, I fancied a llama's curiosity, I imagined life on the trail without freeze-dried food, I dreamed gourmet. The next day, I began planning a trip with the boys from Hurricane Creek.

I was not disappointed.

We - eight llamas, ten hikers, and Stanlynn - started the following May in ninety-degree heat. A week later we finished in a blizzard. The variety of temperatures and terrain irrevocably convinced me that hikers and llamas make a winning combination.

Now my dreams have names attached and photos to match - Pardner eating my apple at lunch, Levi whining when his pals got out of sight, Murphy toting the ice chest and cook box without complaint, Coyote dawdling, Pal spitting, Billy blithely peering over the dropoff on Devil's Staircase, Cupcake stopping at every dung pile, Pard stepping out after passing two lady elk, Billy bucking, Murphy rolling, Coyote munching on purple flowers, Pal devouring the tree to which he was tied, Levi cutting switchbacks, Bandit sitting down in the heat, Billy sitting down in the snow, the packer laughing every step of the way.

Packing with Llamas is a great way to meet these new hiking companions of mine. In its pages you'll not only find vignettes of their travels, but you'll discover how to choose a pack llama, how to care for him, how to train him, and what to expect from him on the trail. You'll learn about llama equipment, llama diets, llama health, and llama idiosyncracies. You'll also pick up some tips about gourmet trekking and even about starting a commercial pack business. While the latter information may not mean much to you now, wait until you own your first llama or two. I expect you'll soon want more.

In fact, by picking up this book, you've already taken the first step toward llama-love. So whether Stanlynn Daugherty's pictures attract you, or her descriptions entice you, or some special llama on a trail somewhere has captured your heart, welcome to the back-country world of *Packing with Llamas*.

(Ann Ronald is Professor of English, University of Nevada, Reno. Author of *The New West of Edward Abbey* and editor of *Words for the Wild,* she has been involved in leading trips for the Sierra Club.)

Preface to Fourth Edition

In 1989, when the first edition of *Packing With Llamas* was published by Rosana Hart and Juniper Ridge Press, there were few resources readily available for people interested in hiking with llamas as pack stock. Now, nearly ten years later, there's a lot more information out there in the form of books, videos, training seminars and packing events. In the last two decades the pack llama has gained solid recognition, and llama packing is a growing recreational activity.

Since 1994 the Backcountry Llama Rendezvous has been an annual event held in varying locations in three western states. Llamathon endurance races in Colorado and California, have tested the limits of what fit and well-trained llamas can achieve. The "Classic 2000" pack llama has been featured in shows and sales in Idaho. The number of U.S. Forest Service districts using llamas in the backcountry is on the increase throughout the west, and the Forest Service, in cooperation with the International Llama Association, has conducted scientific studies of llama trail and grazing impacts in the backcountry.

Many llama breeders are devoting their breeding programs to producing strong, athletic llamas with performance as packers in mind. Members of the Western Idaho Llama Association spawned the Pack Llama Trial Association which has developed a standard and a format for testing the training and performance of the pack llama, and at the same time created an enjoyable social and educational opportunity for llama packers to get together. Pack Llama Trials are now being held all across the U.S.

It's wonderful to see how the pack llama community has matured, and it's been fun and exciting to participate in the process.

When the Dal Porto family at Clay Press, Inc. offered to bring *Packing With Llamas* back in print I was excited and heartened. It gave me an opportunity to update this book with what I've learned since the earlier editions, as well as continue to provide a solid reference for new llama packing enthusiasts. Some chapters such as Selecting a Pack Llama, Equipment for Packing, and Training Your Pack Llama have been highly revised and, I believe, improved. I guess there's nothing like experience to learn from and be guided by. I hope my experiences can be useful to others.

Llamas have brought many wonderful experiences and people into my life, and I feel blessed. I am very grateful to cheryl and Cleave Dal Porto for their support, their commitment to keeping this book in print, and especially for continuing to make *Llamas Magazine* a quality forum for all camelid enthusiasts, including those interested in llama packing. My friend Marty McGee never ceases to amaze me with her insight and compassion for our four-legged companions. Through her wisdom I have enriched my relationships with my llamas, and I hope I have shared some of that in these pages. There are people who have worked hard to ensure pack llamas their place on public lands and they are rarely acknowledged. So I'd like to especially thank Scott Woodruff and Jay Rais for their tireless efforts in this regard—I believe that everyone reading this book owes these two a debt of gratitude for their accomplishments. Thanks also to Noel McRae, editor of *The Backcountry Llama* and author Gwen Ingram for their contributions to sharing information among llama packers, including an excellent reference for llama evaluation included in this book.

People often ask me about the specific llamas that are mentioned and pictured in this book. Murphy is, at this writing, nearly nineteen years old and still a willing packer, as is Cupcake, only one year his junior. Both pull double duty, serving as teachers for the novice packers I train each year. Llama Levi is now spending his days guarding a flock of sheep, turning over his place in the string to younger and fitter packers. His old amigo, Coyote, met his demise several winters ago when he chose to lie down under the wrong tree during a wind storm. Veteran packer Pardner is also retired now, and is happily grazing in the back pasture. I'm hoping I can find a home for him as I did for past packer Palouse, who now lives with a herd of horses, allowing them to become accustomed to the sight and smell of a llama in preparation for meeting one on the trail.

Taking the places of the retired packers are the young upstarts. This year it will be Billings, Beamer, Pim, and possibly Pearl, my first female pack prospect. While I'm happy that most of my llamas are seasoned trail travelers, I look forward to what I'll learn from these rookies. Those experiences are, for me, what makes packing with llamas so much fun, mile after mile.

Stanlynn Daugherty
Wallowa County, Oregon

Chapter One
WHY PACK WITH LLAMAS?

T he trail climbed steeply up the ridge line. The hiker behind me, leading a llama laden with a colorful pack, observed that the path wasn't designed for easy hiking - even the switchbacks we encountered were just there to get around vertical rock outcroppings. In between gulps of rarefied eight thousand foot air, I answered that this trail had been made nearly a hundred years ago by herders pushing their bands of sheep up to the alpine meadows for summer grazing.

I looked back down the rocky path. Nobody had to push my llamas. If anything, their nimble motion was encouraging the group of tired hikers. One of my younger llamas was balking a bit at a switchback - he would learn a lot this trip. None of the llamas had any real difficulty negotiating the uneven terrain, but they were visibly laboring under their loads. We had ascended over two thousand feet in just about two miles.

Above me I saw the arms of an ancient white bark pine that had long ago been the victim of a lightning bolt. This snag marked the top of the ridge, and I hollered back words of encouragement that we were almost there.

A few minutes later, we were walking on level ground. Before us, the basin opened up into a vast meadow filled with wildflowers and

The basin opened into a vast meadow filled with wildflowers.

crossed by a clear, meandering stream. In the mud along its bank, there were footprints from an elk that had paused for a drink earlier in the day. The llamas grabbed mouthfuls of wild onion, as they started to cultivate the aroma that would linger on their breaths for the next three days.

Our campsite was just ahead, on a rocky knoll with a full view of the basin and the surrounding serrated ridge lines. Perched above the granite boulders at the upper end of the basin, another mile by trail, was the destination for our next day's hike, a small cobalt blue lake that was home to some very tasty little brook trout.

But now it was time to relax. We unloaded the llamas, and turned them loose with their picket lines in tow; later we would picket them securely. They rolled vigorously and began hungrily to devour the onions and the meadow grass. They suddenly seemed to be filled with energy. Perhaps they had the same feeling that I used to have when I took off my heavy backpack, a sensation of being so light that I could almost fly.

It was wonderful to see how the eight llamas blended into the backdrop of the meadow, so naturally at ease in their mountain surround-

In camp, llamas blend into the mountain backdrop.

ings. It even looked a little like the Andes, here in the Wallowa Mountains of eastern Oregon.

As we ate our lunches, we looked forward to spending the next three days relaxing and exploring the area. Thanks to the efforts of our llamas, we would enjoy a few extra comforts and culinary delights that we wouldn't have been able to haul up the ridge on our own.

How lucky we were to have such an opportunity to experience the magnificence and serenity of nature at her best.

Fresh air, the scent of the woods, sparkling clear streams and lakes, enchanting meadows brimming with wildflowers, sunset's last glow on the mountain top - all these and more invite us to escape our workaday worlds, stretch our muscles, and recharge our spiritual batteries.

The joys of outdoor recreation have found a place in the lives of many Americans. Local parks, beaches, national forests, and remote wilderness areas beckon. Modern innovation has created a plethora of high-tech camping and sports gear for every recreation opportunity. But one of the most exciting innovations in backcountry travel is the growth in popularity of the llama, an animal who has been carrying burdens in South America for more than six thousand years.

Introducing the llama

The llama has often been called the "truck of the Andes." The great Inca empire was built on the backs of llamas carrying goods through rugged mountains. Century after century, caravans of llamas have transported salt, grain, and root crops to trading centers throughout the Andes. In addition, the animals have provided meat, wool, and fuel for the Indians of the region. Even today, llamas serve remote areas of Bolivia and Peru, where the Andes Mountains restrict other forms of transport.

This animal is totally adapted to mountain travel. Its unique foot consists of two tough, fleshy pads with a curved toenail at the end of each one. No shoes are necessary to protect this remarkably durable foot, though most llama owners provide occasional toenail trimming. These feet, combined with a natural grace and agility, allow llamas to travel through rugged terrain where other pack animals might have more difficulty.

The calm nature of experienced llamas on the trail makes them safe for hikers of all ages to handle. When startled by a flushed grouse or some larger animal, they will often take a short defensive jump and then stop to assess the situation. They are not prone to bolt in blind terror.

Llamas' low cost of maintenance and ease of care allow them to find homes with people of all means and levels of experience. Llamas take to their task naturally, quickly learn to load into a vehicle, and seem to truly enjoy the new sights and smells of backcountry excursions. The way they meet a hiker at eye level makes them genuine trail companions.

Their size, an average pack llama weighs between three and four hundred pounds, is very manageable and not usually intimidating to beginners. Because llamas are limited to loads that seldom exceed one hundred pounds - not more than fifty pounds on each side - people need not possess mighty muscles to handle packing chores.

Who packs with llamas?

Anyone who has ever shouldered a backpack has at one time or another wished for help in bearing the load. Many llama owners today are former backpackers, some of whom are no longer able to carry as much in their own pack, due to back or hip problems. Also, backpackers often find the llama's low environmental impact appealing.

Llamas are genuine trail companions.

A pack llama can be the perfect solution for families with young children who otherwise would have to limit their outings to day hikes or car camping. Kids and llamas are naturals together. Trained llamas may easily be led by the youngest of hikers, and some llamas have been taught to accept a saddle and a small child as a rider.

Backcountry photographers have found they can trust llamas to carry an array of expensive equipment into remote areas. They may take a wider assortment of heavy camera gear, gaining more photographic options, versatility, and mobility. Some commercial llama packers offer trips designed especially for outdoor photography enthusiasts.

Llamas make excellent pack animals for crews maintaining wilderness trails.

Llamas are being used to carry gear for Forest Service maintenance crews that formerly backpacked all their equipment into the woods. In addition, llamas played a vital role in building the 469-mile Colorado trail, hauling food and supplies for the construction volunteers.

The sharp eyesight and hearing of llamas, along with their alertness, lead them often to spot wildlife and other travelers on the trail well before their human companions. Many hunters have discovered this to their advantage when packing with llamas. Hunters also like the ability of llamas to pack game out of rugged areas where horses or mules would have difficulty.

Llamas and other pack animals

Compared to horses and mules, the more traditional pack animals, llamas seem to come up short in one important area. They can't carry

Trained llamas are easily led by the youngest of hikers.

as much. You'd need at least two llamas to carry what an average mule would tote. Even the diminutive donkey can easily carry more than a llama can.

But the utility of a pack animal is not completely measured how much it can carry. Llamas may carry less than mules, horses, or donkeys, but they are also easier to care for, transport, and pack.

In camp, llamas require minimal care. Move their pickets twice a day, offer them water and supplemental feed morning and evening, and they are quite content. Other pack animals often require additional feed which must be packed in on their backs.

The smaller size of llamas is definitely an advantage in getting to the trailhead. Two llamas can be transported in a small pickup, while one horse requires a larger truck or a horse trailer. I can haul up to ten llamas in a sixteen-foot stock trailer that would hold half as many horses.

Techniques for packing the llamas are simple and easy to master once you learn the basic principles of saddling and balancing loads. Most llama packs are designed for quick loading, and do not require complex knots or hitches.

Llamas are less expensive to maintain than mules or horses, and while you may need two llamas to carry what one mule will, you will be feeding them only half of what that single mule would eat. Because their feet are covered with a tough pad, llamas don't need any extra footgear; you will not have any farrier bills to pay, as you would with horses and might with mules and donkeys.

Another benefit of llamas' padded feet is that they are less dangerous to work around than any hoofed animal. A well-placed kick from a mule - and they often place them well - can break a person's leg, or worse. Llamas don't kick very often, but over my years of working with them, they have kicked me a number of times. All I've ever received is minor bruises on a few occasions. I've never been bitten by a llama or seriously injured in any way from their actions.

Llamas are quite easy on the environment. Their unobtrusive dung pellets are virtually odorless, resembling those of elk and deer. They rarely kill the plants they eat, preferring to nibble a morsel here and a bite there. And llama footprints leave perhaps less impact than Vibram-soled hiking boots, and certainly less than the tracks of heavier, hoofed pack animals. In many instances, National park and forest service officials have occasionally allowed llamas into fragile areas that are off limits to horses and mules. Llamas leave little more trace of their visit to the wilderness than elk do.

I can't say enough about the intelligence of llamas. They learn tasks quickly and use good sense when encountering obstacles. Their intelligence is complemented by their curiosity and the keen interest they show in new surroundings.

With all of these traits and six thousand years of experience, it's no wonder that ever-increasing numbers of llamas are taking their place in the backcountry along with horses, mules, and donkeys. Llamas fill a unique niche among pack animals.

Purposes of this book

This book has been written from the point of view of an experienced commercial llama packer writing for prospective or new llama owners who want to pack with their animals, but it's also written for anyone with an interest in these fascinating creatures.

If you're considering llama packing, this book will give you insights on selecting animals and equipment, caring for llamas at home and in the backcountry, and training pack llamas. If you already have experience in packing with llamas, you'll read about another packer's methods and learn what's involved in starting a commercial pack business. If you are just discovering the world of llamas, you'll find plenty of basic information and stories.

All readers may find something of interest in the appendices which list llama publications, organizations, training clinics, as well as equipment manufacturers and suppliers. Other appendices list a few favorite recipes for backcountry meals, a pattern for sewing a basic set of llama pack bags, a list of some poisonous plants, and a checklist for llama buyers.

Of course, there is no substitute for experience - many things you just can't learn from a book. Weather and trail conditions may often present challenges. Emergencies, whether llama or human, can arise. The stories and information in this book are designed to assist you in preparing for llama packing, to make it all the more likely that you and your woolly friends will have a safe and enjoyable backcountry experience.

Cost analysis for prospective pack llama buyers

Llamas: Trained, $1,000-$2,500. Untrained, $400-$1,000.

Pack system: $250-$500

Halters, lead rope, picket, buckets, brushes, nail clippers: $50-$75

Annual feed and routine vet care: $85-$150 per animal per year, depending on local feed prices and amount of pasture.

Transportation: Small truck, van, or trailer. Do you already own or will you need to purchase?

Pasture and housing: Minimum one-half acre, fencing, and a small shed for shelter. Do you already own, or will you need to lease or purchase?

Chapter Two
SELECTING A PACK LLAMA

S ince the 1970's there has been a tremendous growth in North America's llama industry. Llamas are now being raised in nearly every state of the United States, province of Canada, Australia, New Zealand and several European countries. While llamas are still most abundant in the Western U.S., they are rapidly growing in popularity in other regions as well. Estimates of the North American llama population in the late 1990s were upwards of ninety thousand animals. You may not have to go far nor pay a fortune for a packing partner.

Shopping philosophies

What really makes a good pack llama? This is a question I am frequently asked, and I still ponder it myself. As llama packer and also a pack llama breeder, I'm directly concerned with how to create a pack llama from the get go.

When you set out to buy a pack llama, learning what to look for and locating such a critter is your primary concern. In many regions there is an abundance of male llamas potentially suitable for packing from which to choose. How do you make the best choice?

Indulge me for a paragraph or two while I draw an analogy between llamas and autos. There are many different models of cars, and people buy according to their feelings about performance and appearance. It's the feeling part that seems to require emphasis. If any car will get you from point A to point B in about the same amount of time, why are there so many models to choose from? Of course some are more comfortable and some focus on economy. Some have more room for luggage or passengers, others look very stylish. People are willing to pay extra for whatever features they feel they need in the vehicle they drive.

While on one level I'm not so eager to compare an animal to a machine, it seems we can make many of the same points with llamas. Most can be trained to carry a burden on their back, but do you really want a Porsche to take you over the back roads of Idaho? Do you require the features of a one-ton, flat bed Ford in order to enjoy your occasional family weekends in the woods?

So, to begin, I encourage you to decide what your packing needs are and then look for a llama to fit the bill. What do you desire from your four-legged hiking companion and what type of animal will fit your needs? Are you planning long distance hikes, or long summer weekend trips? Do you need llamas to pack out big game or carry your toddler? Are you willing to pay more for the extra features you want (training and experience)? I suggest that you should be prepared to - while good packers may be found in the back pasture that doesn't mean they're available at "back lot" prices.

Within the designation of "pack llama" many, but not all, llamas fit the bill. Size seems important to some people. Get a big llama for a big load and he may work out, or he might not have the attitude and may be outperformed by a smaller, more willing llama. A llama that's all business when it comes to packing yet wants only a minimum of interspecies interaction with his two-legged handlers could be a big disappointment to a family with young kids who want more than just a backcountry porter; they want a buddy.

So, the challenge becomes matching your packing requirements with an individual animal. You, as the buyer, must work to match the animal's abilities to your needs.

As a buyer of a pack llama, what can you do to get what you want? The answer may be as simple as asking for it. However, in order to ask, first you have to know what you want. Yes, you want a "good packer", but how old and how trained, and what will your actual packing demands be?

Jumping back to the auto analogy again - when you're looking for a new car you don't usually go to an auto auction, so it's probably a good idea not to buy your first llama, especially a potential packer, at an auction. As a car shopper you customarily take one or two Saturdays and spend time kicking tires at the car lots, listening to a lot of, well let's just call it information, and taking a few models out for test drives. Purchasing a pack llama can follow the same idea. The big key is to locate llama breeders that actually have pack llamas for sale and then arrange visits to see what they have to offer. This may take a little leg work.

Be aware that many llama breeders have little or no packing experience themselves, but they will usually have males for sale that they believe would "make a good packer." That is ultimately *your* decision.

A good place to start your search is in the classified ads of llama publications or regional llama association newsletters, and the internet has numerous llama home pages as well. See the appendices in this book for lists of llama organizations and llama periodicals.

Make a point to schedule your visits when both you and the seller have plenty of time; you don't want to rush your evaluation process. Appendix Eight contains a checklist for buyers. You may want to take a copy along to refer to when shopping for your packer.

Sexual Preferences

Traditionally in North America, male llamas have been used for packing. For many years the value of female llamas kept them off the trail and in the breeding pasture, producing more little llamas. More recently, an abundance of llamas and a drop in prices has led to more females being trained to pack.

At this point I guess I should mention a journey I made a few years ago to the *Hautes Alpes* of southern France where I was lucky enough to hike for seven days with a pleasant group of people and llamas. As if hiking in the French Alps wasn't unique enough on it's own, the trip was also notable for the gender of our llamas - two of the string were females.

At the risk of sounding like an advocate for female llama equal rights, I'm starting to think that more lady llamas should be put to

Lady llamas can pack their share. On a hike along a country lane in France, Appenzelle brings up the rear.

packing use. Certainly the performance of the females I've packed with on two separate trips to the French Alps has shown me that they can do the job quite handily.

Without a doubt our two-legged group's favorite llama was a stately eight-year-old female of Swiss origin, suitably named Appenzelle. She possessed a very unique personality, and was given to resting her head on her human leader's shoulder, especially on downhill sections of the trail. She commented softly and frequently on the events of the day, and I held a secret vision that, had she been human, she would have had a definite fondness for costume jewelry and romance novels. Our other female llama companion was more businesslike and often chose to walk near the end of the string.

Two issues around packing with females quickly raise their heads. The first is how can packing affect a pregnancy? On that trip one of the females we led was not bred, the other was pregnant and had already had her last baby weaned. They were both on the small end of medium-sized adults and carried approximately 60 pounds five to nine miles a day. On another Alps trek our female packers were either young maidens carrying very light loads or moms with recently weaned youngsters. My French packing partner, Christiane, has not had any problems with losing a pregnancy in the girls she packs. This all leads me to think that one could probably make a strong case for the benefits of packing as physical exercise for our girls. Many breeders are plagued with overweight females who do little more than sit around the pasture and eat, and the breeders find themselves at wit's end trying to solve the problem.

The second issue that pops up is how might it work to pack females and males together in a string? We used only geldings in the groups we led in France, and we were leading them individually and not stringing them together. Depending on the temperament of the male, it seems feasible that we could have taken a well-mannered stud along as well. It may help if the females were in fact pregnant, and not giving off continuous signals inviting the male to change that status. It's possible that the bigger challenge would be hauling intact males and females to the start of the trek. A divided trailer or van would be the best bet, and a distant second option would be to keep the animals tied during the ride. Unless it's a short distance to the trailhead, keeping llamas tied is always a least favored alternative.

Spaying female llamas, while not as inexpensive as gelding males, is a viable possibility, and new techniques make the procedure a relatively simple surgery. You may want to consult your veterinarian for more details if you have a good female pack prospect and are considering this option.

So, while I as yet have no other personal experience packing with female llamas, I have spoken with at least two other people who have taken their girls into the backcountry with positive results. In both cases they were barren (or thought to be). I'd love to hear from more people who have experience packing "mama" llamas.

It seems that as prices for females drop, the barrier of worrying about taking such a "valuable" animal into the backcountry must drop as well. Eventually an animal's price must reflect its useful value and what better way to assess and assure the fitness and vigor of the animals we breed, both male and female, than to give them first hand experience on the trail, performing tasks as their ancestors have for thousands of years?

With the case made for females, I now say that unless you intend to breed llamas and are willing to invest the additional money in a breeding-quality male, then I recommend looking for a neutered or "gelded" llama. Gelding is a relatively simple surgical removal of the testicles, customarily performed under sedation by a veterinarian. While llamas may be gelded as young as five months, it's better to wait until they are at least 18 months to two years of age.

All baby llamas are adorable. At this age, it is difficult to tell what their adult size and build will be. Looking at their parents will give you good clues.

I like to wait to geld until I see the fighting teeth beginning to emerge from the llama's gum line. Studies have indicated that the surge of the hormone testosterone promotes emergence of the fighting teeth, and also coincides with growth plate closure in the legs. Earlier gelding *may* prevent full closure of the growth plates and compromise the structural integrity of the llama's legs over time. The studies are not conclusive, however. So, unless the llama's behavior is a management problem, I like to wait for the teeth to emerge before gelding, just to be on the safe side.

In making your pack llama purchasing decision, some more points to consider are the animal's age, build, personality, level of training, and health.

Age

If you want a llama that you can begin packing right away, look for one at least two years of age. Younger llamas do not have the stamina for strenuous pack trips, nor is it advisable for them to carry much weight while their bones are still forming. I've seen adult llamas that began packing before the age of two who later developed leg problems. It's possible that these were caused by carrying full loads too early. Even two-year-olds' loads should be kept very light.

If you wish to raise and train the llama yourself, then choose a younger fellow. Llamas are weaned between five and six months of age. They may be taught to accept a halter, to lead, and to be loaded into a trailer or low vehicle at that time.

Keep in mind that many qualities you will be looking for in your mature packer are less developed in a younger llama. By age two the animal will be more physically mature; you will have a better idea what you are getting. Almost all young llamas are cute and fuzzy - nearly irresistible. Then, like teenagers, they go through an awkward stage. Between the ages of six and eighteen months, their faces lengthen, they may lose their baby fuzz, and you see the final llama beginning to emerge. Males begin reaching sexual maturity at eighteen months or later. Llamas are deemed fully mature at four years of age.

I'm often asked, "how long can llamas pack?" In 1998 I spent my fifteenth summer on the trail. Two of my first llamas, Cupcake and Murphy, were right there with me, at ages 17 and 18 respectively. I packed them a bit lighter than I had during their early years, but they covered a couple hundred trail miles. I have also retired llamas at younger ages.

Occasionally a llama will develop a weakened ankle or a chronic lameness, or he may just lose his desire to work. Aptitude, genetics and conditioning all play a role in determining the useful life of a pack llama. My experience has led me to believe that one who passes these tests and stays healthy should pack well into his teens.

Build

Llamas come in all shapes, sizes, and colors. Remember the end use and ask yourself if the llama you are looking at appears able to eventually carry fifty to a hundred pounds of gear up to your favorite alpine lake, or perform whatever tasks you demand. The shape of his ears will have little to do with his willingness and stamina.

The initial concept in visually evaluating a llama is one of "balance". The basic elements of this balance are the ratio of leg length to back length to neck length. On a well-balanced llama these will be

Evaluating llama conformation starts with looking at the animal's balance and proportion.

relatively equal. As you look at many llamas you will often see animals with proportionately shorter necks to the length of the back. You will also run across those with short legs relative to back or neck length. A well-balanced, well-proportioned llama will have a higher likelihood of fluid gait and ease of movement.

You want a substantial back to place your pack on. Look for a straight and perhaps slightly short-coupled back, rather than one that is rounded, swayed, or proportionately longer-bodied.

Some breeders may say a wide chest makes a good pack llama. I think they believe he will have more lung capacity. I have found that many llamas with very wide chests walk laboriously, with more difficulty than average-chested animals. This gait will cause the pack to sway from side to side more than is desirable, making it more work for the llama and difficult for you to keep the pack balanced. This is not to say that I look for a narrow chest; I like something in between. Again, the key is balance and proportion.

Of course good, sturdy legs are very important. As you look at them from both the front and the back, they should be straight - not bowed, nor turned in or out at the knee or the hock. Straight front legs are the same distance apart at the feet as they are at the chest. A long leg may mean a longer stride and short work of the miles between the trailhead and journey's end. I like to see a llama with good straight leg, of a length in proportion to the rest of him, that shows obvious muscle on the inside of the foreleg.

Finally, have a look at his feet and ankles. When viewed from the side the angle from the back of the foot up through the ankle joint to the lower leg should be no more than about twenty-five degrees off vertical. If there is severe angulation at that joint, the llama may have what is often referred to as "dropped pasterns" or weak fetlocks. This is a very weak joint and not something you want to see in a pack llama.

Avoid a llama with weak pasturns, as shown here on an older animal.

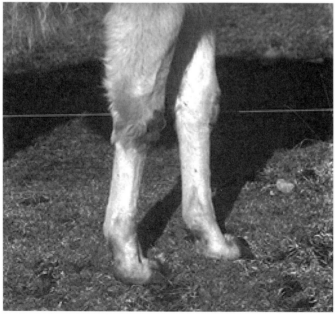

Look for good, sturdy legs with upright pasturns, as shown here.

Spend some time watching the animal move both on and off the lead. Are there any signs of lameness or an awkward gait? Most llama breeders won't try to sell you a lame animal, but some injuries could go unnoticed. Look for any odd bumps or markings on the llama's legs, possible signs of a past injury, but don't be confused by the hairless, dark patches of skin on the inside of the lower back legs. Resembling a chestnut on a horse's leg, these are normal. They are commonly referred to as scent glands, but their function is unknown.

Hands-on evaluation

Many llamas have been fed a lot and exercised very little. As a result, they are fat. As they have a coat of wool to cover it up, it's hard to tell for sure just how much fat is there. So, as much as possible, get your hands on the llama you're looking at. Once you're a llama owner you're going to be evaluating your animals' fitness, so use your purchase examination as an opportunity to begin learning how different individual llamas feel.

Start by feeling down his spine from behind his neck to his mid-back. Just behind the withers along the llama's topline, you should be able to feel the spine and a slight indentation down either side before it widens into the top of the rib. You want to determine the slope of the angle from the top of the spine down over the lumbar muscles, with approximately 45 degrees below horizontal being good for a fit llama. You'll feel more flesh on plumper llamas, and if you can hardly feel the spine, you're dealing with an obese llama.

Another place to feel for extra flesh is in the relatively wool-less area on the llama's side, just behind his elbow. You should be able to feel a rib or two. If you can't feel ribs but you do feel lots of flesh, he's packing extra fat.

In the chest area you'll feel lots of extra fat if he's got it, however if it's well filled out but firm, that's more muscle than fat.

In the "ham" area of his rear legs you'll want to see some space between the upper legs of a llama in good shape. If he's got "thunder thighs", he's overweight. In this condition, it will take a lot of work to get him into shape for packing, but it's not necessarily a reason to pass him by. Just remember that the more extra weight this llama carries in the way of body fat, the less athletic he'll be, and the less of your gear you can put on his back until you get those pounds off.

Keep looking at and feeling the body condition of as many llamas as you can until you are comfortable distinguishing the different points of conformation and levels of conditioning. If this is a new topic to you, it can be helpful to take along someone who knows horse or other livestock conformation. Their more experienced eye may see structural faults that you would overlook. If you have a friend who knows llama conformation take them shopping with you.

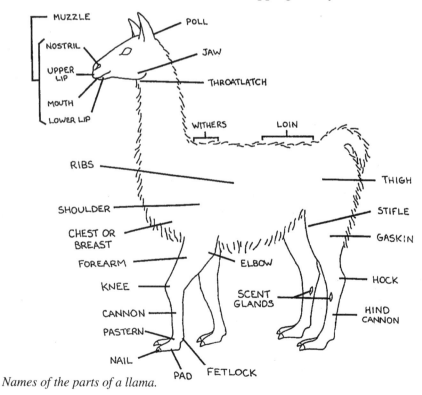

Names of the parts of a llama.

Personality

While there are exceptions, llamas are generally somewhat aloof. In a herd of llamas, each individual has his own personal space and repels any intruding llama by raising his head, pinning his ears back along his neck, and threatening to spit.

That leads to the most commonly asked question about llamas: "Do they spit?" Yes, llamas will spit, most frequently in the course of food disputes, dominance wrestling matches, and sometimes when confined together in the small space of a trailer. Female llamas will spit when refusing the amorous advances of a male llama, or when defending their young. Llamas will spit on humans when they are feeling threatened or in pain. Some of my llamas will spit when being given an injection, or when being sheared. As normal, well-adjusted llamas, they do not spit on me when I catch, halter, or pack them. Llamas that have been spoiled or poorly handled may spit at the slightest annoyance. Avoid these animals at all costs.

The actual substance the llama spits may simply be the hay in its mouth at the time of provocation. If seriously agitated, he or she may regurgitate and spit additional stomach material. Contrary to rumor, it will not cause blindness if some of it lands on your eye. Being spat upon is painless, though smelly.

When you approach a llama, it may retreat several steps, usually stopping at a distance just beyond your arm's length. Even if a llama will come up to take an offering of grain or fruit, it will often move away should you reach out to pet it.

Don't take this behavior too personally. Unlike horses who will spend time head to tail enjoying mutual grooming by scratching each other, adult llamas together in a field will avoid physical contact with each other.

Llamas have a basic instinct to flee a situation they perceive as threatening; running is their primary, instinctive defense. With time, trust, and training, this instinct can be overcome. However, it is something of a paradox that an animal which looks so cuddly does not seem to enjoy physical affection.

With this knowledge you can understand why experienced llama owners will counsel new buyers to beware of an excessively "friendly" llama, one that immediately runs up to the fence and sticks its nose in your face. A normal llama may come up to investigate - perhaps in search of a food treat - though typically stops short of you by a little distance. A llama who comes too close, especially one that quickly has his head out to sniff your face, toes or your crotch, does not have the proper respect for your personal space. He could be a big problem, especially if he has "imprinted" on humans.

Imprinted llamas may behave toward people as they would toward other llamas. Imprinted males can be dangerously rough, attempting to wrestle and even show dominance or breeding behavior toward humans. These traits are sometimes known as the "berserk male syndrome". It is not something that can be untrained; a number of male llamas have had to be euthanized because they were simply too dangerous to be around humans. If the llama you are looking at shows any aggressively friendly traits, don't buy him. Also, I strongly recommend that no new llama owner purchase a llama that was bottle-fed, as bottle-fed males are more likely to develop these problems.

If the llama you are considering is already halter-trained, he should follow you willingly on a loose lead. Balking, lying down, or spitting during haltering or leading are signs of an ill-trained and possibly maladjusted llama, one that you should not consider purchasing. Don't be tempted to buy another person's problem just because the price is low.

Obviously, weanlings and untrained llamas will be more of an unknown quantity. Their behavior at first handling may be a reaction based on fear and inexperience rather than unwillingness. In many cases, you will have to be guided by your own intuitive perceptions of these animals.

Training

If you're a novice packer it's probably better not to start with a novice llama as well, so your quest is to find a llama that's trained to be easily caught and haltered, that leads readily, and that has had at least initial pack training.

However, there are a lot of folks who either fall in love with an untrained llama or feel they want the full training experience. If that's your story then be sure you seriously consider how confident and willing you are to take on training chores. If you have previous large animal experience you may feel fairly confident about taking on this new challenge. Recognizing that llamas are not horses, you will need to learn a bit more about their special psychology in order to match your training methods with their learning abilities. Several training practitioners offer clinics that can teach you how to teach your llamas. Check Appendix Seven for a list of trainers providing this service.

While llamas learn quickly, they are just as apt to learn the wrong thing as the right one, so you will need to be committed to the task of training a novice packer. Fortunately, llamas are somewhat forgiving. Everyone makes mistakes in their initial llama training efforts, but rarely is a llama ruined by an honest, if imperfect, attempt at teaching him to do basic packing chores.

To help facilitate your training, one option is to purchase a well-trained, seasoned packer along with a younger, inexperienced llama. The experienced packer can serve as a role model and a valuable instructor for the younger one. This option gives you a chance to possibly save some money over the cost of two seasoned packers, and to enjoy the experience of training a llama yourself.

Once you've located a good prospect that's being sold as a "trained pack llama", it's quite reasonable to ask to halter the llama, or to be instructed in how to properly halter him.

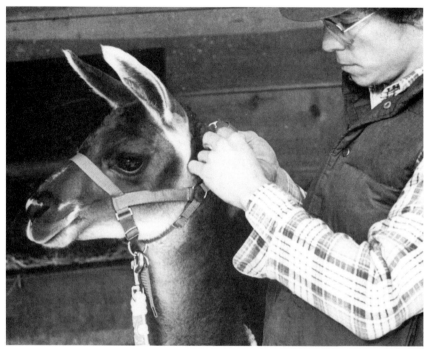

A trained llama should be easily caught and haltered, and should show signs of a pleasant disposition.

I know that many first time buyers are shy about what they don't know (I was that way at first, most people are), but do as much as you can to put that to one side in order to learn and make a better decision about your purchase. You should also be able to observe saddling or, with assistance, saddle the animal yourself as well as put an appropriate load on the llama. If the llama is being sold as "experienced" then you, even as a neophyte, should be able to get a halter and saddle on it, and thereby make a learning opportunity out of the evaluation of the animal for sale.

This is your "test drive", make the most of it. Don't expect to go four-wheeling though. Unless you're actually going out on a pack trip, you'll probably be limited to taking a hike around the confines of the seller's ranch.

The seller should have a vehicle or trailer for hauling llamas, so don't miss an opportunity to see how easily the llama loads inside. It's yet another piece of information that will help you evaluate your potential trail companion's performance of standard tasks.

Throughout this process you should be looking at the llama's behavior He should be easily handled and certainly not spitting or kicking. You should be asking questions about his age, when he was trained, how much, if any trail experience he has, if (and when) he's been gelded, if his fighting teeth have been trimmed (they should be if he's over three years of age), and if he's ever had any illness or injury.

How easily is he caught and haltered? While llamas do have a tendency towards aloofness, it can be mellowed with time, trust, and consistent handling. It's okay if his ears are back at first, but they should come up as you walk out across the pen or yard. Ears back, head up and threatening to spit - or actually spitting - is not an acceptable combination of behaviors in this situation.

Will the llama allow you to pick up his feet? Llamas are very sensitive about this, and many good pack llamas don't stand calmly for it. But if he does, he's just earned more respect. Are his toenails trimmed? If someone is selling you a prize packer at a prize price, the animal should show signs of excellent care and maintenance.

The wool factor

The length and type of wool varies considerably from one llama to another, and presents some points to consider when choosing a pack llama.

Llamas customarily have two types of fiber; a coarse outer "guard hair" and the softer, finer, undercoat of wool (that, when spun, can make lightweight and wonderfully warm garments). The guard hair helps the llama shed rain, snow, wind and debris; wonderful attributes for packing. Some llamas bred for finer wool will actually lack or have very little guard hair, which allows debris and weather to become factors in the care and use of the animal.

Some llamas have abundant wool on their back, sides and rear, while their neck and legs may have very short (1-2 inches) wool. Others have a very wooly neck, rear legs and even cheek and forehead wool. I shear nearly all of my pack llamas, so the length of body wool becomes a neutral factor, however it is more work to shear a wooly neck and keep abundant leg wool tidy. Consequently, I, along with many other breeders of pack llamas, aim to minimize the wool on the animals I produce, and to breed llamas that have abundant guard hair.

A llama's performance may be affected by its wool length if you live or will be packing in a hot climate. A wooly llama will be more sensitive to the heat, tiring more quickly than shorter-wooled llamas; this makes shearing a true necessity, even for relatively short wooled llamas. Some people say that dark colored llamas suffer more than lighter ones, but heat sensitivity seems to depend on the individual animal's tolerance and conditioning, rather than its color.

For years I avoided llamas with an excess of wool, and certainly didn't add any wooly females to my breeding herd. Then a few years ago a wooly male caught my attention with his size, his grace of movement, and his distinctive persona that never fails to bring a smile to my face. (*Everyone* should have a llama that makes them smile often.) I was lucky enough to add Piero to my herd and, even though he was seven years old and had never even seen a pack saddle, he quickly learned the packing routine and became one of the most proficient packers I've ever led up the trail. He has sired several babies for me now, not all of them have his abundant wool type, however thankfully all have his size and grace. Today I'm still less drawn to a

Piero and friend prove that, when sheared, wooly llamas can be fine packers.

wooly llama as a packer, though I'm always willing to look at the whole animal when making a purchase evaluation, weighing each element in relation to the others.

Health

When evaluating a llama you're thinking of buying be sure to ask when he was last wormed, what vaccinations he's had, whether he's been gelded, and if so, when. If part of the pasture is swampy, ask if the ranch has had any problems with liver flukes. These are most commonly found in wet areas where cattle have been pastured. You should ask if the llama you're looking at has ever been sick or injured, and if so, the circumstances involved. Even if you aren't sure how that would affect him, you can find out by consulting a veterinarian. It is good to have the information for possible future reference.

I am not the only llama owner who could have saved herself some heartache by being more thorough. Paco was one of the first llamas I purchased. Although I didn't find out when I bought him, I later learned that he had a history of choke, a condition in which the esophagus becomes easily blocked. He tended to gobble his hay pellets rather than chewing them thoroughly, and they would lodge in his esophagus. As these pockets of food enlarged and blocked his esophagus, he would try unsuccessfully to regurgitate them up. I had to take him to the vet to remove the blockage several times over the course of two years before he ultimately died of inhalation pneumonia associated with his condition. Neither the seller nor I realized the long-term problems Paco's condition could cause, but a veterinarian might have warned me about this relatively common livestock disorder.

Now, when I do feed supplemental pellets, I spread them through the hay, rather than making tidy little piles for each llama to wolf down. When I feed them by hand or during training, I make sure the llama takes one or two mouthfuls, then I remove the pellets until he's had a chance to chew them thoroughly, before offering more.

It's always a good idea to have a veterinarian check any animal you are serious about buying. The seller no doubt has a vet who knows about llamas and can give an accurate assessment of the animal's health. A vet check should include listening to the llama's heart, taking his temperature, examining the llama for external parasites, and observing him visually for soundness.

There is no standard procedure regarding who bears the cost of the exam. Often a willing seller will do so. Or, as a buyer, you may wish to think of it as buying short-term insurance that your purchase price will be partially protected from any obvious and immediate health problems. You may split the cost with the seller, and you may choose to make the sale contingent on the animal receiving a good "bill of health" from a veterinarian before taking ownership.

How many llamas?

Early in your plans, you'll need to consider how many llamas you'd eventually like to have. It's important to realize that llamas are social, herd-oriented animals. They are better off living with other llamas. I firmly believe that this is a serious consideration, especially if you are buying a very young llama. Llamas can become lonely without the social interaction that's important to them.

I know of a nine-month-old llama that was sold to a couple in a nearby town. After a week of being pastured alone, he jumped the fence and took off, seemingly in search of other llamas. The couple spent a frantic afternoon before finding him and bringing him home. Once back in the pen, he jumped the fence again. This time it took the help of many friends to catch him. The couple eventually returned him to the farm where they bought him, and left with a low opinion of llamas in general. This was not an isolated incident; I have heard a number of similar stories about lonely, single llamas.

Individual llamas have been successfully raised with other animals such as sheep, goats, and horses. Since these animals are also herd-oriented, llamas are commonly able to adapt quite well to their unconventional pasture mates.

But be careful if you should want to board your llama with horses. The horses may dominate the feeder and prevent a llama from getting enough to eat. A llama's chief defenses are spitting or running away, while a horse may be prone to attack with its sharp hooves or its teeth. An aggressive horse could seriously injure a llama. If you choose to have llamas and horses together, watch their behavior closely and make certain that they are able to coexist peacefully.

Owning at least two llamas has some definite advantages. On the trail, two llamas can carry twice as much gear with little extra care. Two llamas may as easily be kept in the same area as one, and they will enjoy each other's company. Two llamas can be transported in most pickups as easily as a single llama. And llama owners will tell you that, like potato chips, it's hard to stop with just one.

Under average circumstances, the cost of keeping one horse is equal to keeping three to four llamas. While buying another llama adds to

Individual llamas have been successfully kept with other animals, such as sheep, goats, and horses. A lot depends on the personalities of the animals.

the initial investment, the general cost of feeding and vet care for a llama is low, so having two shouldn't be an overwhelming expense.

Perhaps you have some friends who share your enthusiasm for the idea of llama packing. You might consider purchasing a couple of llamas together and rotating weekends for llama excursions.

Throughout the book, I'll often be talking about one llama. This doesn't mean I'm advocating having just one - I'm simply talking about one at a time.

Some other considerations

Don't make price your highest priority. If the price is high, you should expect some extras along the lines of training, experience and a guarantee. Paying extra for fancy bloodlines on a pack animal is only reasonable if the bloodlines are those of outstanding performance or pack animals. If the price seems remarkably low, be straightforward about asking why. Some breeders end up with an abundance of males which they sell at low prices to move them off the farm. Others sell cull animals at a low price, so you should carefully scrutinize any animal that seems to be a bargain. The buyer should definitely beware in any purchase of livestock.

If you are purchasing an untrained animal, you will have to rely on his overall physical condition and your gut feelings about his potential. Look at the ranch in general. Do the animals seem healthy? Are fences in good repair? Is the owner sensitive to your needs or just trying to get rid of extra male llamas? How does the seller regard his llamas - as pets, working animals, "investment" livestock? Does the seller show the desire to place the llama in an appropriate situation, or the desire to move it off the farm? Which kind of llama would you like to own and which kind of seller would you like to buy from?

After your evaluation process and hopefully a "test drive", you'll have a feeling about the animal that will have something to do with his appearance and performance, but it will also have a lot to do with another kind of connection that we develop with animals (human and otherwise). Just as with people, we relate to different personalities in different ways. With some people it's easy to be on friendly terms very quickly, others seem harder to get close to. And just as we can often forgive some friends' faults while enjoying their positive energy, we can overlook some llamas' weak points because other aspects of their personality are so appealing. With pack llamas it's really easy to forgive less than perfect looks and perhaps smaller size if they seem to show a lot of willingness and heart for hiking.

I truly believe that any experienced llama packer will say that willingness is the most highly sought after quality in a packing companion. The only way to really judge that is to get the llama out on the trail. All the training in the world won't be much help for a llama that simply doesn't have the heart.

Since you most likely won't have a chance to take your potential purchase out for an extended pack trip until after you buy him, you run the risk of getting out there and realizing that you and your llama were not such a good match after all. Let's go back to asking for what you want (the most you'll get is a "no" - and that's more information). Some sellers, I hope I'm not the only one, will give you a month or more after your purchase in which to make the final evaluation - is this the llama for me? A seller that's just as concerned with a happy buyer and a happy llama as he or she is with a happy bank account is worth looking for. As buyers, you have an opportunity to ensure your own success as well as that of the seller by asking for and not taking advantage of such an agreement.

There may also be opportunities for you to lease a prospective purchase for a packing season with an option to buy him at the end of the summer. This would be another way to really be sure you won't end up with a "lemon".

In your quest for the perfect pack llama be sure to have an idea of what you want and then seek it out. There are a lot of llamas being sold as packers that may not really be suited to the task. While it's hard for lots of us to be severely analytical of an animal, certainly more so than we could be of a machine, you're going to have to live with your purchase. You're the one ultimately responsible for your decision no matter what the seller says. That's why it's important to get your hands on the animal and, as best you can, see what he can do. Take time to learn at every opportunity so that you can make an informed decision. Don't forget to trust your intuition, as that can be a valuable part of your final analysis.

Llama relationships

I heard a great story a while back - one that illustrates a lot of things including why I love packing with llamas, what a difference a good pack llama can make, and what unique characters our llamas have.

At the time of this story llama Pillsbury was a four year old male owned by Rocky and Jerrie Hammons of Meridian, Idaho. That year the Hammons took Pillsbury on his first backcountry journey into the rugged Seven Devils Mountains on the Idaho side of Hells Canyon. He was in a string of five other llamas, each of them somewhat seasoned packers.

On this trip the Hammons family packed in eight miles and camped out two nights before heading back home. On the way out Rocky put Pillsbury in the front of the string and began the eight mile hike back to the trailhead where they'd begun their journey. Heading up a series of switchbacks Amante, the llama just behind Pillsbury, started "dogging" - not keeping up - and pulling on the lead rope connected to Pillsbury's saddle. This behavior made leading a lot more work for Pillsbury, and he handled it well, continuing to follow Rocky up the trail. Finally, Amante lay down, too pooped or too uninspired to continue.

What happened next surprised Rocky and caused me to chuckle when he told me: Pillsbury turned around to face the reclining llama and lashed out with his front foot, striking Amante two times in the chest. Then he vigorously spit in Amante's face. Obviously Pillsbury had had enough of tugging this loafer up the trail, and now he was letting him have it. Amante got up immediately, and for the rest of the journey followed Pillsbury up the trail with slack in the lead rope.

Now, I certainly don't want to endorse physical violence as a solution to any situation, however these llamas had their own communication going on, and it was what it was. The fact that Pillsbury obviously took it upon himself to deal with the situation, and the results were such that the string continued to hike out a reasonable distance under a reasonable load, leads me to allow that this individual llama had the head and the heart of an exceptional packer.

While we're telling stories . . . I have observed other llamas interact in "unusual" ways. In one instance years ago, I rescued two adult male llamas that were both not gelded, and had been fighting with each other for quite some time. Riley was bigger and more aggressive, and had done physical harm (torn ears at minimum) to smaller Sherman. I kept them separated for the first few days after they arrived, and made an appointment to geld both of them as soon as possible. On the day the vet arrived I put Riley in one corral and Sherman across the fence in an adjacent corral. As sometimes happens Riley went down immediately after his shot of sedative, while Sherman seemed unaffected. When Riley hit the dirt Sherman saw his opportunity, leaned over the fence and promptly plastered Riley with the biggest blast of green spit I'd ever seen. While it seemed to me a minimal payback for what Sherman had endured, it surely appeared to be given in that spirit.

Certainly not all llama behavior that we can translate into human perspectives is negative. Many times llamas create a bond with one another that really seems like "best friendship." Sometimes I feel this when I see two llamas that do especially well hitched together in a string, graze together in the pasture, or take special notice and sometimes hum when the other is taken out of the field and separated from the group.

I've also been pleasantly surprised to see llamas connect with people in a very short time. On one learn-to-pack trip where the participants were given a llama for their own to handle for four days, I witnessed my llama Cupcake bond with his human companion. At one point on the last day's hike out we took a break along the trail. Shortly after we started hiking again, Cupcake's human realized that he'd forgotten his hat at the last rest stop. We stopped along the trail and he went back to retrieve his hat. It was a drizzly day and as he disappeared into the fog Cupcake looked back and gently hummed for the few minutes it took the fellow to locate his hat and return. I was impressed and somewhat surprised to notice this behavior. I guess I attribute it to the ability of the human to connect with Cupcake, as well as the willingness of Cupcake to relate to this his handler.

I don't spend a lot of time anthropomorphizing my llamas' behavior. I'm just telling you what I've seen and what I've heard. There's no question that these animals are intelligent and that is one of the reasons people are attracted to them, whether packing with them or enjoying them in other ways. As with individual people it's easy to connect more with some llamas, while others are more challenging to work with. That's no doubt why we have our favorites. There's certainly something to the fact that we meet these animals for the most part at eye level and this quality, as well as their individual characters, make them outstanding packing *companions.*

Chapter Three
FEEDING AND HEALTH CARE

S ince you will be investing considerable amounts of time, money, and emotion in your pack llama, you will want to give top priority to feeding him and maintaining his good health. Don't try to trim expenses by falling behind on vaccinations or wormings, or by purchasing cheap and possibly inferior hay.

Fortunately, llamas are very thrifty animals - they prosper without excessive amounts of expensive feed or extra special care. Many owners spend less than one hundred dollars per year to feed and provide veterinary care for each llama they own.

What to feed llamas

Llamas graze on grasses and forbs (non-grass herbs), and they browse on trees and shrubs. A llama may be somewhat selective as to what suits his palate, but keep in mind that bushes, flowers, and vines are all fair game to a llama.

Llamas are very efficient in their digestive process, much more so than a sheep, cow, or horse. Classified as modified ruminants, llamas digest their food in a unique, three-compartmented stomach. You will often see llamas chewing their cuds.

What and how much you feed a llama should depend on his current condition, the season, and his level of activity. Basically, good grass or oat hay, mineral salt, and fresh water will fill most of the llama's needs. After consulting with your local vet or extension agent, you may want to consider additions to his diet such as vitamin, mineral, and protein supplements. These options will depend primarily on the nutritive quality of your local pasture and hay, the age of the llama, and his condition.

Look for grass or oat hay that has been well put up so it's not moldy or bleached out, that has been stored under cover, and that contains between eight and ten percent protein with approximately forty percent fiber content. If the seller doesn't know the nutritive content of his hay, you may want to check with your local extension agent concerning feed analysis. It's not expensive; the price probably varies from area to area. My extension agent looked at my hay, and without any questions told me where it was grown and how it was put up - I grew it, so I knew he was right - as well as the relative protein. He also told me how to improve my crop.

Good hay, salt, and fresh water fill most of a llama's dietary needs.

In most instances, alfalfa hay is overly high in protein and calcium for a llama's needs, and may place a burden on the animal's metabolism. Remember, these creatures evolved in the highlands of South America, thriving there on low protein grasses and forbs.

Overfeeding will result in a fat llama, one that will have less energy and take more time to get in shape for pack season. A good guideline is to feed no more than 1.5% of a llama's body weight per day. That's about five pounds of hay for a 350 pound llama who is not also grazing on pasture. If he weighs 350 pounds but is somewhat overweight (use the hands-on analysis described in the previous chapter to assess his condition), use your best judgment in lowering the amount of feed to accommodate his ideal weight. Nursing females, just-weaned babies, and thin llamas should have their ration increased to closer to 2% of their weight. During harsh winter conditions you may need to supplement all llamas' normal rations with additional hay or a bit of grain.

Be sure your llamas have access to water which is freshened daily and to free-choice salt. While many prefer granular to block salt, you might want to offer some of each at the beginning, to learn their preference. I put out both kinds, using salt that contains supplemental trace minerals formulated for my area.

One trace mineral very important to your animal's health is selenium. If lacking selenium, animals can suffer from a condition called white muscle disease and possibly die.

Adequate amounts of selenium are lacking from the soil throughout large parts of North America. In these areas, the hay and pasture grasses are not going to provide enough selenium. If you live in a region deficient in selenium, be sure to offer a feed supplement which includes it. You may also choose to give an annual injection of selenium. I live in such a region, and consequently I make sure my llamas have a granulated mineral supplement with selenium available to them "free choice" throughout the year. Several brands of supplement formulated for llamas are available across the country, and simple trace mineral salt with selenium is also available.

Be aware that excessive amounts of selenium are toxic. Some areas have an excess of selenium in their soils. If that is the case in your region, you certainly would not want to give any additional selenium to your llamas. . While supplements are formulated with this in mind, it's a good idea to consult your local veterinarian before giving llamas any selenium supplementation.

Feeding a herd

If you have several llamas, you will surely notice that some of them eat more than others. Just like people, some llamas like to eat a lot while others seem less interested in food. Some of your llamas may put on a lot of weight during the winter as they lounge about the feeder. Others may need supplemental feed to keep them from losing weight during the colder months.

The ideal way to monitor your animals is to weigh them. If you do not have access to a scale, pay close attention to how your animals look and feel. You might find it necessary, as I do, to divide your llamas into the fatties and the skinnies, place them in separate fields, and ration their feed accordingly.

On the trail

When llamas are being heavily used during the packing season, they may require supplemental rations. Out on the trail, I feed a mixture of half alfalfa pellets and half C.O.B., a common horse feed consisting of corn, oats, and barley enhanced with some molasses as well as some extra vitamins and minerals. I call it "llama granola" and I customarily offer one or two cups per llama as a reward for a good day's work. Your llamas will need more supplement on days when you've traveled long distances and camped in areas with sparse feed than on rest days in a grassy mountain meadow.

Be sure your supplemental feed is processed so you won't be introducing non-native seeds into the backcountry environment. Let your llama eat from the bag, from your hand or a reusable paper plate, avoiding wasting feed spilled on the ground.

Llamas like the extra treats and I like having a bit of time appreciating my animal's hard work and personality. In addition, my llamas have become very attuned to the sound of the Ziploc plastic feed bag. I find this very useful for catching them; whenever necessary I just rustle any plastic bag, and they come to investigate.

If you will be taking an extended trip above the tree line, or through other areas where your llamas will find little grass or browse, you will need to increase the amount of supplemental llama food you carry. For a 350-pound llama, you may need to carry up to five pounds of high energy supplement per day. You can reduce the amount fed if there is some browse available.

To any supplemental feed you take along, you may wish to add an electrolyte replacer and a mineral supplement. Electrolytes are used to maintain the body's chemical balance and are especially important for hard-working pack llamas in hot weather. Loss of electrolytes can cause dehydration, cramping, and muscle fatigue. You may add one to two tablespoons of "lite salt" to their feed, or you may purchase specially formulated electrolyte replacer from your vet and add it to their drinking water. It is very important that your llama has access to plenty of water when you give him any additional electrolytes.

If your llama granola does not already contain supplemental vitamins and minerals, you may wish to add a half tablespoon of Horse Guard, Northwest Horse Supplement, or other similar product to their

Cupcake accepts a snack from a hiker. After a day on the trail, supplemental feed will nourish and reward your llama.

daily ration. Check to see that the product does or doesn't contain selenium according to the needs of your region.

An excellent, comprehensive pamphlet entitled "Feeding Llamas" is available from the International Llama Association. Its address is listed in Appendix Six.

Health care

A regular health care program for llamas includes annual vaccinations for tetanus and any other local livestock diseases, regular worming for internal parasites, shearing and toenail trimming as needed. Because conditions vary from region to region, you should consult your local large animal veterinarian for his or her recommendations concerning routine veterinary care.

I vaccinate all my llamas annually against tetanus and two clostridial diseases. While popular seven-way and eight-way combinations are available, the extra protection they afford is not a concern where I live, so I use tetanus toxoid and types C and D clostridium perfringens. Your vet can advise you on which vaccine to use where you live. Be aware that it is important to always use a killed vaccine for tetanus shots and that seven- and eight-way vaccines are prone to cause abscesses. More a nuisance than a health concern, you will usually need to treat the abscess if it forms.

Llamas can become infected with most of the internal parasites common to other forms of livestock. For this reason you will want to worm them regularly, to prevent the debilitating effects of parasite infestation. Worming medicines, known as anthelmintics, are formulated to eliminate one or more specific types of internal parasite. It is a good practice to take a fresh fecal sample to your vet in order to identify which parasites, if any, are present. Then you can use a wormer for that purpose. There are several worming medications which kill common parasites and many vets recommend rotating among different ones to prevent the parasites from building up a resistance to a single type of wormer.

You may choose from injectable, paste, liquid, or granular forms. Most llamas won't eat the granular, and the liquid types can be messy to administer. I have had good success with injectable or paste-type wormers for internal parasites.

Llamas can get lice, both biting and sucking types. If you discover hair loss over the withers, across the chest, or near the tail, or if you notice a llama scratching or rubbing these areas excessively, you should examine him thoroughly for tiny lice. Your vet will be able to make recommendations regarding treatment; it varies depending on the type of lice. Llama lice are not transmittable to humans.

You will need to trim your llama's toenails if they grow out faster than they wear down. Using anvil type pruning shears available at garden supply stores, trim the toenail even and on the same plane with the bottom of the foot pad. Training your llamas to allow you to pick up their feet will make this task easier. If you trim too short and draw a little blood, don't be alarmed. The toe will quickly heal and shouldn't cause lameness.

How often you need to do this will depend on the surface the llama has been walking on, and how much exercise he's been getting. In the summer, my llamas are on the trail regularly, and they keep their toenails worn down on their own. In November, and every two or three months thereafter, I check my herd and trim as needed.

If you buy an animal without a preliminary examination, be sure to take it to the vet soon after you bring it home. This will give you a chance to meet your vet under pleasant circumstances, allow you to bring your llama's vaccinations up to date, if necessary, and give you some additional peace of mind. It is helpful to take in a fresh fecal

This llama's toenails have been trimmed even with the bottom of his pad, using anvil pruning shears.

This llama, a two-and a half-year-old male, has fighting teeth that need to be trimmed.

sample at this time or even before the visit, so that your vet can check for internal parasites. If the llama has been pastured in a swampy area where there is potential for his having contracted liver flukes, be sure and alert your vet to this possibility.

Llamas grow a set of six fighting teeth, two on either side on the top of the mouth and one on either side on the bottom, which are most pronounced in adult males. These teeth can cause injury as llamas play and wrestle in the course of normal herd interactions. The teeth should be cut off at the gum line after they erupt, between the ages of two and three. This is a simple procedure that can be done using an obstetrical wire saw with adequate restraint and most often without sedation. The llamas really don't seem to feel much pain from this. This technique is sometimes demonstrated at llama conferences. If you have two or more male llamas, I highly recommend that you be sure their fighting teeth are removed, to prevent accidental injury and possible disfigurement.

You should have a good idea of how much your llamas weigh in order to give proper dosages of vaccinations and worm medicines. Many llama owners do not have livestock scales but occasionally take their animals down to the local feed store to be weighed. It's fun to let the customers have a guess before leading the llama onto the scales. Most of them are amazed at how little the llama weighs - his wool cover can be deceiving. The serious side of this is that even highly competent veterinarians can guess wrong if they are not familiar with llamas, and an error could result in an incorrect dose of important medication.

In addition to weighing, an analysis of excess body fat along the spine, lower rib, chest and rear leg "ham" area is recommended. The procedure is described in the preceding chapter. I like to record both weight and this "body score" using relative a 1 to 10 scale with 5 designating an optimal fitness condition.

If a llama seems to be losing weight or body fat without cause, be sure to have him examined by a vet before you start pushing the extra feed to him. He could have a health problem that is not immediately apparent. Check his health record, paying special attention to when he was last wormed.

Llamas are extremely stoic animals and will rarely show signs of illness until it is well advanced. So if you happen to notice any indications of possible ill health in a llama, be sure to monitor the situation closely. It's better to get help too early than too late. While they are very hardy creatures, llamas can have a variety of health problems not outlined here.

Llama organizations keep lists of veterinarians who are available for consultation regarding llama health concerns. Please note that they will consult with other veterinarians rather than with llama owners.

Grooming for packing

Removing excess wool from your llama will keep his coat healthy and make your regular grooming chores easier. Friends of mine who pack horses and mules wonder how I ever get the wooly coats of my llamas brushed clean enough to saddle. Horse packers are used to making sure their animals are thoroughly groomed so that nothing is under the saddle blanket where it could cause a sore. While it is true that llama wool picks up a lot of debris, it's not really a lot of work to keep them tidy enough for packing.

These days I shear most of my packing llamas and some of my females. The undercoat of wool on a llama, unless removed, can matt and prevent good air circulation to the skin. Not only does this make the animal retain body heat that may build up during exertion, such as carrying a loaded pack up a mountain trail, but it's also less healthy for the skin. Brushing is one way to remove the loose wool, but it is time consuming and not very comfortable for the llama.

Shearing keeps your llama's coat cleaner and reduces his risk of overheating during summer pack trips.

In the spring or early summer, I trim my llamas' wool down to between one to two inches in length. After shearing, it's much easier to keep the undercoat brushed out and the llama clean. There won't be problems with long wool getting tangled in cinches, and the llama is much more comfortable and able to perform better on the trail during the hotter months. If I have a chubby llama, I may trim him as early as March, when it's still fairly cold. With a lighter wool coat he'll burn extra body fat to keep warm.

Some folks use sheep blocking shears to cut their llamas' wool. I've had more success with a spring-loaded "scissor/shear" made by Fiskars, and have also used heavier electric shears. It's important that the blades on your shears, be they hand or electric, are very sharp to avoid pulling as they cut. The suppliers listed in Appendix Seven sell all types of shears, as do most farm supply stores.

Most llamas don't enjoy the shearing process, so I make this a two-person operation whenever possible. The helper keeps feeding the llama treats, and we work in a small catch pen so the llama has the freedom to circle around a little while I shear. Starting at the top line, I cut a swath along the spine. Then I work down, from front to back or back to front, depending on which side of the llama I'm on, always cutting in one direction. I also trim the wool under his belly, as that's an important area for ventilation.

If you're working alone, you may need a smaller area and a way to keep food in front of your llama. If he seems especially stressed by the procedure, break it down into two or three shorter sessions, and try not to lose your temper. Remember that this is not natural or comfortable for your llama.

Don't despair if your llama looks like a punk rocker when you finish. Give him a light brushing, and then go back and trim the longer spots. Just like for people, the difference between a good haircut and a bad haircut for a llama is about two weeks.

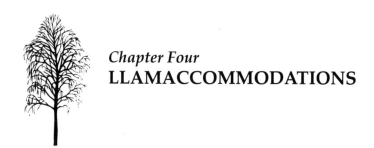

Chapter Four
LLAMACCOMMODATIONS

O ne of the great things about owning a pack llama or two is that you don't need a large acreage to pasture them comfort ably. With a sturdy fence, a small barn or loafing shed, and a fresh water supply, you can easily keep two llamas on a half-acre parcel of land.

Even in northern winters a three-sided loafing shed is sufficient protection for a healthy llama. He'll use it more if he can sit inside, out of the elements yet able to see what's going on. You need enough area under cover to keep your llama's feed dry and to allow him to get out of the rain, snow, or wind. If you do not have any trees in your pasture, he may use his shed for shade as well.

If you will be building from scratch, your local extension office is a good place to look for livestock housing plans and ideas. It's easiest for you if you can store hay near where you feed, so allow extra room inside under cover.

Llamas like their personal space when eating, so don't try to crowd too many at a short trough. Allow at least three feet of trough for each llama. I've discovered that if I make the roof over the feeding area no more than about eight feet out from the wall, my llamas will not usually start a dung pile underneath.

Llamas tend to establish certain dung piles in their pasture, and then they will go to those piles. This means that if a pile isn't present, when you're hiking or if you bring a llama into the house for a short visit, they tend to wait a while before starting a new pile. Where they live, they will only rarely start new piles.

Llamas will also create a dust wallow somewhere in their pasture. They enjoy grooming themselves by rolling vigorously in the dirt. In my fields, I have several areas where I burn fallen cottonwood branches in the spring. The llamas have appropriated these for their wallows. They use them the most in the heat of summer, when the flies are the worst.

If you live in a climate where the water will freeze during the winters, water trough heaters or heated, insulated buckets, commonly available through feed stores, will save you some trouble.

Fencing

Llamas are very easy animals to contain, provided they are fed, watered, and not lonely. They do not lean on fences like horses or cows do, though they do like to stick their heads through pole or wire barriers to graze or just to see what's there.

Most types of fencing four feet high will contain llamas; some llama owners use up to six feet for additional protection against heavy snows or neighborhood dogs. It is more the height of the fence and less the material it's constructed out of, that provides the barrier to the llama. Your choice will depend on your pocketbook, your neighborhood, and what is already in place where you plan to keep your llama or llamas.

Many llama owners, including myself, swear by New Zealand style, smooth wire fence. My own fence is partially electrified to keep out the neighbor's cows. Though it is not dog-proof, it could have been constructed that way had dogs been a concern. If dogs do run loose in your neighborhood, take special care with your fencing; dogs have injured and even killed llamas. I like New Zealand fencing because my llamas cannot be injured by it, the maintenance is minimal, and the cost to install it was very reasonable.

Woven wire is a dog-proof alternative. Be sure the openings are not large enough for a llama to stick his head through. He could be injured in this way, especially if wearing a halter.

Pole fencing is a good choice for fencing llamas when dogs are not a concern. You can put the poles up unpeeled if you want, leaving the bark for the llamas to nibble on. They will occasionally nibble on the bare poles, but will not eat the wood as aggressively as horses do.

While barbed wire will contain llamas, I do not believe that it is desirable fencing. The barbs can seriously injure you and your animals, and they are not a necessary deterrent. Barbless, twisted wire is a reasonable alternative.

New Zealand fencing, with its smooth wires, is an excellent choice for your llama pastures.

If your property is already fenced with inappropriate barbed wire, don't think you absolutely must go to the trouble and expense of re-fencing before you bring your animals home. Examine your fencing for general safety concerns such as loose or protruding nails. Check for stray strands of wire lying in the fields, perhaps half buried. Then plan to replace sections of barbed wire as time and finances permit.

In designing or adding to your llamacommodations, put in plans for a catch pen and make your life with llamas simpler. When you want to catch your llamas, herding them into this small corral adjacent to your main pasture will save you lots of time and energy. If possible, put their feeding area in the catch pen and it will be even easier to coax them inside. Catch pen fences should be a bit higher than field fences, and poles or bars should be more closely spaced.

If you place your gates in the corners of your field or corral, your herding tasks will be simpler. You'll be able to walk the llamas along the fence line and through the gate.

But don't worry if your existing gates do not conform to this pattern - llamas have a fascination with open gates, especially newly opened ones. They will often walk right through with little bidding. In planning the placement of gates, think about your herd movements and what will make the flow smooth.

Make sure that your pasture has at least one gate eight feet wide or larger. Eight feet is the minimum width that will allow a truck or tractor to pass through. If you will be applying fertilizer or cutting hay in any of your fields, the gate should be at least fourteen feet wide.

In addition to having these larger gates, most of my corrals and pastures allow me to enter by way of what I call a walk-through gate. These small gates are made out of wood, and have a long spring that pulls them closed after I walk through. I build them wide enough for

Loafing sheds provide shelter and an covered feeding area. Small corrals make catching llamas easy.

a wheelbarrow to enter, and I always make them so that the door swings only into the corral or field.

When you visit other llama farms, take a close look at their corral and pasture layout. Ask questions about how they catch their animals and handle their herd movements.

Keeping males together

A group of several male llamas living together form what animal behaviorists call a bachelor herd. The llamas will set up their own hierarchy of dominance. Most likely, one llama will be the boss, and the others will have a descending order within the herd.

Be cautious in introducing any new llama to the herd. He'll need to find his place within the group. It helps if you can pasture a new llama next to the existing herd for a few days, so that everyone gets acquainted across the fence at first. This also gives you a chance to be sure he's healthy. Some people prefer to quarantine a new llama, with some space between him and the home crowd, for up to two weeks, just to make sure.

A newly-introduced llama will have to find his place within the group.

To reach a top position in the herd, a llama will fight and wrestle, forcing underlings into submission. This is natural behavior and a good form of exercise as well. As long as none of the llamas have their fighting teeth and there is sufficient room in the pasture, the animals rarely inflict serious injury on each other.

Fighting male llamas can be noisy. In the course of their dominance disputes, they sometimes make strident screams at each other. This scream is one of several sounds that llamas communicate with. The most common sound is a nasal hum that may indicate a variety of feelings such as anxiety, curiosity, or discomfort. My llamas occasionally hum at the trailhead while we're sorting loads and packing up. They usually stop as we begin to hike.

The llama's alarm call is a distinct noise that sounds to me like a cross between a horse's whinny and a rooster's crow. It is made when a llama notices something threatening nearby, like a strange dog. My llama Billy would give this call if he saw horses in the distance when he was in camp. When one llama gives an alarm call, all the others immediately look around to see what's happening. Occasionally llamas will give the alarm call at the behavior of another llama.

If male llamas, either gelded or intact, are living out of sight of female llamas, they aren't usually too serious about their dominance struggles. If one llama is the boss, the others won't get in his way at the feeder, but neither will he try to run them out of the pasture.

Everything gets more intense when female llamas enter the picture. If you will be breeding llamas, you will need separate pastures for the males and the females. If you have more than one stud, it will work best to pasture them out of sight of the girls when they're not breeding. If this isn't possible, you may need to separate your studs. It all depends on the individuals involved.

Male llamas will challenge each other in the course of their herd interactions. Here they are playing "King of the Hill" on a snow pile.

In one pasture, I keep a bachelor herd of up to twenty geldings and one or two studs. They all have to pack together so I want them to work out any differences on a daily basis, not on the trail. When my females are in the field across the street, the males stay pretty quiet. The studs simply have their own spots on the fence where they look longingly at the distant pasture. Occasionally they strut, snort, and strike masculine poses.

Two of the older geldings are higher up in the herd order than the younger studs. These geldings rule over the feeder but don't care so much about the fence line. Now and then, one will challenge a stud. The fighting males may rise up on their back legs, bumping chests and screaming. Usually it's over in a few minutes.

In the spring, I move the males into the large back pasture where they can get some exercise and enjoy the fresh green grass. Sometimes I will bring two or more females that are due to have babies soon in a field closer to the house. Now the males are in a field adjacent to the ladies, and the dynamics change considerably. The oldest stud takes up the fence line position, and heaven help any other llama that dares approach it! He runs off any male that comes near.

This works out because the males are in a sixty-acre field. Everyone lets the stud have the fence; they still have plenty of room to roam. If they were in a small field, then things could be very different. Aggressive males, both studs and geldings, have been known to keep other, usually younger, fellows in one corner of the pasture, usually the farthest from the females. Aggressive males may become quite violent in challenging each other. If this persists, then separation of the aggressor may be necessary.

No llama owner likes to see excessive fighting in their herd. The sound of screaming males is not pleasant. But hormones are definitely a factor, and depending on your pasture arrangements, the llamas will eventually work out their own order. Do make sure all your llamas' fighting teeth are trimmed!

It's important to note that aggressive intact males will not undergo an immediate transformation if gelded. While it will take time for the hormone levels to change, it can easily take more time, perhaps a number of months, for behavioral patterns to adjust.

Watching the interactions of your llama herd is one of the most interesting parts of being a llama owner. Each herd will have its own unique dynamic, and there are no hard and fast rules. Positions of dominance may change, and geldings may be dominant over actively breeding studs.

One summer long ago, Cupcake had the uppermost position in the herd. An older gelding, he was small and domineering - a real Napoleon. Whenever I returned other males to the pasture after hikes, Cupcake put his ears back and charged aggressively at the newly-released animals. I didn't like it, but there wasn't much I could do about it. He was one of my best pack animals, so getting rid of him was out of the question.

Then I bought Billy, another small, feisty llama. He didn't take any guff from the others, but he didn't provoke them either. He seemed to disapprove of Cupcake's actions as much as I did. Billy placed himself between the just-released llama and Cupcake, and he gave Cupcake a defiant look that said, "Go ahead - make my day!" Cupcake paused. The newly released llama ran off. I observed Billy doing this several times; eventually Cupcake lost his urge to harass the others.

You might wonder how such a llama got a name like "Cupcake." He was a real terror when I bought him as a three year old, one of my first llamas. He was hard to catch and hard to halter. I couldn't pick up his feet without a rodeo, and he wouldn't stand to be brushed. He wasn't the best animal to be a first llama, but I learned a lot. One of the things I learned was to think positively.

In a conversation with a friend, I said that I didn't have a good name for this llama yet; he was such a jerk that I was tempted to name him "Expletive Deleted," and call him E.D. for short. I was even tempted to call him the expletive. She said, "Why don't you call him `Cupcake' and maybe he'll sweeten up?"

I thought, "Why not indeed?" So I tried it, and it worked. As soon as he got the pack saddle on and his load in place, he was the model pack llama. He was not overly fond of passing horses on the trail, but he did it, and he followed willingly behind whoever was leading him. On my trips he became the favorite of the little kids and the grand-mothers. He gets called "she" a lot, but doesn't seem to mind as much as I do.

Cupcake taught me that llamas learn from the example of other llamas. One day, before I had taught him to jump up into the pickup, he watched a friend's llama perform the feat. Then he jumped right in. Over time, he has come to let me handle his feet and brush him. I have learned to allow Cupcake his little idiosyncrasies; I wouldn't trade him for the world.

Cupcake patrols the fence between the pastures of male and female llamas.

Chapter Five
TRANSPORTATION

How are you going to get your first llama home? How are you going to haul him out to the trailhead? When it comes to transportation, llamas have some advantages over larger pack animals.

Vehicles

Llamas may easily be transported in a pickup equipped with a stock rack or canopy, or even in the back of a van. They will also ride in a small trailer that can be towed behind a compact car.

Most commercial packers, and llama breeders who transport several animals at a time, use livestock trailers, usually between twelve and sixteen feet long and often with a gate dividing the trailer into two sections. This gate is very helpful if you have to haul males and females in the same trailer.

How many can you haul?

Two llamas will fit snugly into a van or compact pickup bed with a stock rack. Three may be transported in a full-sized pickup bed if it is fully enclosed so that they may ride without being tied; other wise, you'll want to haul just two and follow the precautions described later. Two llamas will also fit nicely into a two-horse trailer; three will fit if you remove the stall divider. Some llama owners transport one or two llamas in small single axle trailers they have purchased or built to tow behind their compact cars.

I use a sixteen-foot stock trailer to haul as many as nine adult llamas. It has a center divider that separates the trailer into two sections. If I'm hauling just two or three llamas, I put them in the front section, so most of the weight will be over the tongue of the trailer. If I haul males I know may fight in close quarters, I put them in separate sections.

Safety

If you will be using an open trailer or truck with a stock rack, it is important to have a roof of some sort - something which will make it impossible for a llama to jump out. Side panels on your truck are not only a safety measure but also a good wind break.

If your stock rack or trailer lacks a roof, then be sure to tie your llama, using a quick release knot or device. Leave enough rope for him to sit down and still have his head in a comfortable position, but not enough rope to get tangled up in. One foot of lead should be plenty, and will make it so that he can't jump out. If you are hauling two llamas in the same open truck, it is especially important to tie them so they will not tangle their ropes as they jockey for a comfortable position. Many llama owners transport llamas in enclosed vehicles only, as generally the animals are more comfortable and safer there, where they needn't be tied at all.

While I don't recommend it to everyone, a few times I have transported a small llama in a Subaru station wagon. It has to be a llama that is trained to kush, or sit down on command. I had done this half a dozen times when I was feeling frugal and not wanting to make a long trip in my gas-guzzling pickup. Then one time, I hauled a young female to a neighboring stud for breeding. As we drove down the highway at fifty miles an hour, she tried to stand up. She had enough force to pop out the back window, which shattered as it hit the highway. I wasn't far from home, so I turned around and went back for my truck. So much for saving money.

I submitted the claim for the broken back window to my insurance agent, and we had a little fun with it. A couple of weeks later, the company's claims adjuster phoned to verify the wording of the claim.

"It says here, 'mid-sized llama in compact station wagon.' Is that correct?" he asked.

"Yes, that's exactly what broke the window," I said.

"Okay. I just never had claim like this before," he replied.

I received a check in the mail a week later. Since then, I've traded my llamamobile in on a newer model Subaru - one that probably won't be hauling llamas.

Weather concerns

Llamas need protection from the elements, hot or cold, when traveling long distances. If it's cold and rainy or snowy I want them in an enclosed trailer or canopy on my pickup. Remember the wind chill factor. Side panels or a cover over your pickup's stock rack are recommended in these conditions.

In hot weather protection from direct sunlight as well as good air flow are essential. If you have a trailer, make sure it has adequate ventilation for summer trips. On journeys during really hot weather, it helps to get an early start, planning to reach your destination (or take an extended break) by the hottest part of the day. You may also wet down the floor of the trailer to take advantage of the cooling effects of evaporation - just make sure you have good air flow so you don't compound a heat problem by adding excess humidity.

A small pickup with a stock rack can transport two llamas. Pardner and Cupcake are tied for their short ride to the trailhead.

Other details

Llamas will get hungry on long journeys, so if we are going more than a short distance, and I'm using an enclosed vehicle or trainler, I put in a small flake of hay for them to nibble on. But don't leave water out as you drive along - it's too likely to make a mess.

Most llamas kneel down after you've traveled a mile or two, so a rubber floor mat or a piece of old carpet will make them more comfortable. Avoid using hay or straw as bedding if there's a chance it will blow into the llama's eyes during travel.

On long journeys, you may use the dung-piling habits of the llama to your advantage. Bring some pellets of llama manure with you from home, in a coffee can. During rest stops, unload the llama and give him a chance to stretch his legs. Then pour a few pellets out in a discreet spot, and allow nature its course and the llama his relief! If you stop at the same rest stop on your return trip or on another journey, don't be surprised if the llama remembers the dung pile. Depending on the location of your rest stop, you may want to bring along a rake to disperse the droppings.

If you will be crossing state lines, you should be aware that many states want you to have a current health certificates; for each llama, and possibly proof of certain inoculations and tests. If you want to find out about this, your veterinarian can contact the State Veterinarian of the appropriate state.

Llamas are easily taught to load into a trailer or low vehicle. This can be one of the first lessons you give your new llama; you'll find out how to do it in Chapter Seven, Training Your Pack Llama.

One spring two friends and I hauled six llamas over six hours to take a four day hike into the Hells Canyon on the Idaho side of the

Llamas can be trained to jump into the back of a pickup. Since this stock rack has no roof, Murphy will be tied securely before transport.

Snake River. The trailhead is only 45 air miles from my house, how ever the deepest gorge in North America presents a substantial travel barrier, so we had a scenic, if winding drive.

Along the way we stopped for a lunch break in a nice picnic area at the Nez Perce National Historical Park headquarters along the Clearwater River. I took the llamas out and tied them to a railing next to the trailer where they could graze a bit of grass that the mower had missed. During lunch a Park Ranger walked by and was very interested in the llamas and our trek. As he left he informed me that technically I should have a grazing permit from the National Park Service to allow the llamas to eat the tall grass around the fence posts. He didn't feel the need to say any more, and it was enough to remind me that it's always a good idea to know the regulations for the public lands that we all use, even the edges of a parking lot.

Once we arrived at our trailhead, we met up with three more friends who'd driven over from eastern Idaho. We decided to walk in just a mile to the first creek to make our camp. The llamas seemed confused about the whole process of making the long ride, then loading up and leaving so late in the day. They hummed frequently as if to let me know that this wasn't our usual routine. They made the short hike in fine time, were fresh and ready to go the next day, and they made no complaints during the rest of the trek.

Coming back home after the trip we stopped for gas in a small town alive with a county fair and carnival. It was really fun to observe the llamas, who spend 99% of their lives in a rural or wilderness setting, lean their leads out of the trailer and stare incredulously at the masses of people and carnival rides across the street.

Traveling with llamas can be fun and rewarding for all as you and your critters experience new sights and sounds along the way.

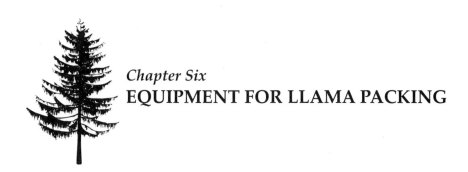

Chapter Six
EQUIPMENT FOR LLAMA PACKING

O nce you've found your packing companions you'll be faced with the task of outfitting them for the trail. In addition to buying some basic gear for trail excursions, you'll need to purchase an appropriate pack saddle system for your llama. Appendix Seven lists llama equipment manufacturers, and most will send you a catalog with descriptions of their wares.

Llama pack systems

Llamas require pack saddles designed specifically for them, because their backs are shaped differently from mules' or burros'. Since llamas are smaller and their loads weigh less than those of equine pack stock, their pack equipment is lighter in weight and construction.

Llama pack systems consist of a saddle, secured by two cinches, and two pack bags, often called panniers, that are attached with straps or buckles. A more elaborate system may hold the saddle on the llama more securely by using additional straps: a breast collar and either a rump strap, called a britchin', or a crupper that fits under the tail.

Most llama pack saddles fall into one of two basic categories, the frame pack or the frameless "soft" pack. The main differences between the two types are their construction and the method used to support the load on the llama. New types of saddles are also being made that incorporate an internal frame in a mostly soft pack.

A frame pack saddle is usually made out of lightweight aluminum, wood or fiberglass and supports the load on the llama's back by distributing its weight over an area on either side of the spine. Horse packers have been using variations of the frame pack saddle for a long time. The frames may be either rigid, with no possible adjustments of the shape of the saddle, or flexible, pivoting to allow for narrower or wider animals' backs. The frame pack saddle is designed to be used with a saddle pad to cushion the frame on the llama's back.

Llama soft packs are most often constructed out of leather or nylon and also have some type of thick, dense padding on either side of the spine to distribute the load's weight on the llama's back. A saddle pad is not customarily used with a soft pack.

Choosing and fitting a pack saddle

When selecting a pack saddle for your llama you should keep in mind the type of packing you will be doing. If your llama will be wearing its pack for showing, parades and an occasional picnic hike you do not need the elaborate systems that will be more functional for someone who is going to travel on rugged trails or into the backcountry for overnight pack trips.

Any saddle you buy should fit your packing plans and, most importantly, it should fit the llama that will wear it. Llamas come in different shapes and sizes, from short and round to tall and thin, and everything in between. Their backs can differ substantially in width or prominence of spine, and they may also have additional bulk from extra body fat. Different models of pack saddles have different shapes. It's critical to match up your system with your llama to ensure his comfort and safety.

Examples of frame pack saddles. The one on the left uses a built-in pad, the one on the right will be used with a small pony saddle pad.

The key elements to a properly fitting saddle are adequate spinal clearance, a means of distributing the weight of the load along the llama's back evenly, and a design that fits the back's contours without restricting shoulder movement.

Most frame pack saddles on the market today have adequate spinal clearance. Some older types may not properly fit a llama with a prominent spine. The width of the side bars on a frame saddle determines how the load is distributed on the llama's back. Thin or narrow bars provide little support. They also run the risk of digging into the llama's side. Wider bars with a way of contouring to accommodate the indentation behind the llama's withers will offer a better fit. In some instances a "corrective" saddle pad that offers additional contour, support, and protection can provide a better fit for a rigid metal frame.

Soft pack saddle systems usually run less risk of digging into a llama's sides or spine, however they must also provide a sturdy, substantial means of distributing the weight of the load along the llama's back, preventing it from simply hanging down on top of his spine.

71

Most do this by means of extra padding along the side, a few inches down from the center of the saddle. The flexible nature of these types of saddles usually allows them to conform to the llama's contours.

You can get a good idea of how your saddle fits your llama by doing the following: Take your llama for a thirty minute hike with a moderate load in the pack. Remove the pack bags, and then carefully remove the saddle (and blanket if it uses one) by lifting straight up off the llama's back. Now examine the wool and note the impression made by the saddle. This is the area where the saddle is making contact with the llama's back, and the part of the llama that is bearing the weight of the load.

First note if the saddle has stayed in place behind the withers and off the shoulder. This is what you want. If the saddle rests on the moving part of the shoulder blade the llama will find it uncomfortable and more difficult to carry the load, and the load is much less stable on his back. Locate the shoulder blade by feeling the llama's back as you place the saddle, taking care to lay the load bearing area of the saddle behind the shoulder blade before tightening cinches.

Next check to see if the wool is evenly flattened along the llama's side (good) or if they are gaps where the saddle was not making full contact, referred to as "bridging" (not a good fit). Areas that are making more contact will compress and may even "swirl" the wool. These "pressure points" will make packing less comfortable for the llama, so padding the area receiving less contact to even out the pressure can help. You may try something as simple as a folded bath towel and lay it on the llamas back to cover the area being "bridged".

Most importantly, check to see that the wool over the llama's spine is not compressed, ensuring that the spinal area is free from contact. A fully loaded pack saddle should have a minimum vertical clearance of one inch over the spine, and three inches horizontally from the center of the llama's back in order to prevent pressure on his vertebrae.

Please note: it's often easier to evaluate saddle fit on a shorn llama in good condition and, most importantly, saddle fit will change if your llama gains or loses weight.

Attachments

All llama pack saddles, whether frame or soft, should have two cinches. The front cinch fastens as tight as possible around the llama's girth, right behind the front legs. The back cinch fastens across the llamas' belly, where it slopes up behind his rib cage and in front of his penis. The back cinch, when fastened, should be snug while allowing you to slide a couple of fingers between it and the llama, about the tightness of a waist belt on a loaded backpack.

Breast collars, britchin's, and cruppers are attachments that fasten the saddle more securely to the llama and keep the saddle in place during steep climbs or descents. Some pack saddle systems include them as standard equipment, others as optional gear.

Saddle systems that use a breast collar and britchin' can help secure the load for travel in rugged terrain.

When llamas are strung together, the pull from a following llama may move the saddle back, necessitating a breast collar. When traveling off trail up and down hills and over obstacles, a breast collar and a britchin' are necessary.

These attachments should be adjusted loosely enough to allow you to pass your fingers between them and the llama when traveling along a fairly level trail. They should be tightened when hills make it more imperative for the saddle to stay in place. The placement of britchin' should be high enough that it does not interfere with the animal's rear leg movement, and below testicles on an intact male. The breast collar should be across the point of the llama's shoulder and not cutting into the base of his neck.

Panniers

Panniers are usually constructed out of cordura, canvas, or similar heavy duty fabric capable of standing up to rugged trail use. Some have an assortment of compartments to help you organize your gear. Others are simple drawstring bags with a top flap closure.

Examples of three "soft pack" saddles that support the load with padding on either side of the llama's spine.

Rain covers are welcome in a downpour or, as here, in a steady drizzle.

Panniers should be able to be attached high on the saddle and thereby high on the llama's side. They should have compression straps that will allow the bag to be packed compactly, again well up on the llama's side. An arrangement that allows for the panniers to be tied down from the lower portion of the bag, attaching to either the cinches or by use of a strap running under the belly, will create a more secure and stable load. This will make it easier for the llama to shoulder his burden mile after mile. Think about the uncomfortable experience of carrying a fully loaded back pack with loosely adjusted shoulder and belt straps and you get the idea.

It is very important that the panniers fit your llama. If they are too large they can hang down and interfere with the llama's leg movement. I have constructed panniers from a simple pattern that allows me to make them the right size for my various kitchen components. Appendix One contains my pattern, with instructions for a set of panniers designed to fit on a frame pack saddle with crossbars or cantle.

Rain covers are usually sold separately from pack saddles and panniers. Constructed out of coated nylon or other waterproof fabric, a rain cover should be large enough to go over full packs and a top load.

By sending off for information from the manufacturers and equipment dealers listed in Appendix Seven, and perhaps visiting equipment booths at llama gatherings, you should be able to select a pack system to suit your needs. If you meet other people who pack with llamas, ask them what type of gear they use, why they chose it, and what they like and dislike about it. Some packers have built their own customized containers; others have devised specialized methods of attaching coolers to their saddles.

For a more thorough description of saddle fit and selection criteria, I highly recommend *Evaluating a Llama Pack for Comfort and Function* by Gwen Ingram. It is essential information, especially if you are considering making your own pack saddle. Ordering information is included in Appendix Four.

Additional equipment

A picket stake, the swivel type commonly used for dogs, may be purchased from your local feed store, a pet supply store, or a llama equipment supplier. Looking rather like a giant corkscrew, a picket stake will securely hold a llama in most but not all soil conditions. If you're camped in an area where you are unable to get the picket stake into the ground, you may need to tie the end of the rope to a large rock or piece of wood that is heavy enough to prevent your llama from dragging it off.

I make my picket lines out of nylon rope. Nylon is strong, light-weight, and pliable when frozen. Splice two snaps onto the rope, one at each end. You might want to learn how to do an eye splice; it's a handy thing to know. Any book on knots available at your local library can show you how to do it. Clip one end of the rope to the llama's halter and one to the stake and there's your tie-out system.

Llamas have been seriously injured from running full speed and hitting the end of their picket rope. For this reason, many packers use a piece of rubber tubing or shock cord to attach the end of the rope to the picket stake, reducing the abrupt impact.

I make my own lead ropes out of half-inch cotton rope about eight feet long. I find cotton to be gentler on hands than nylon. With an eye splice, I attach a snap to one end.

Llama packing equipment for the backcountry

- Pack saddle and bags, with accessories as desired
- Saddle pad if you're using a frame pack
- Picket stake and twenty-foot rope, one set for each llama
- Extra lead rope
- Extra halter
- Insect repellent
- Collapsible bucket
- Llama first aid items
- Llama granola (pellet/grain mixture)
- Pack scales
- Brush
- Duct tape
- Bungie cords
- Fifty feet of nylon cord
- Bells

In the middle of the rope I insert a handy little gizmo called a rope adjuster, available at feed stores. It has three holes; the rope goes through two, and the third is free to hook back to the halter snap for quick temporary tie-ups, and it's great when using lead ropes to hold up the kitchen tarp in camp.

Picket ropes and leads are available from llama equipment dealers, who also offer a variety of llama halters. Since llama heads come in different sizes and shapes, the most useful halters are adjustable. If your llamas use different size halters, the extra halter you take along should be one that will fit even the largest animal on the trip.

Resist the temptation to leave this extra halter at home. I packed one for two years be fore I needed it. Then one day Palouse - inexperienced and a bit obstinate - was not willing to follow Murphy - more experienced and very strong - over a log. Palouse's halter broke in two places, where the ring attached to the throat and chin straps.

Pal was still barely attached to Murphy. I grabbed the extra halter out of a handy outside pocket of a pack bag, then slipped up to Pal and replaced the broken halter. In minutes we were on our way again.

Horseflies and mosquitoes bother the llamas, at least as much as they bother people, so I always have a can of Deep Woods Off or similar spray and a small container of horse "fly wipe" in my pack. At the trailhead, and again in camp, I try to cover the llamas' heads and legs if I know it will be a bad fly area. If you have worked at desensitizing your llama, it will really pay off at this time. Llamas hate the smell of fly wipe; it is often difficult to cover their heads and ears. This is when the spray comes in handy. Be sure to cup your hand over the llama's eye before you spray, and read the product label instructions for proper use.

If a persistent horse or deer fly is on a llama's face, he probably won't let you swat the insect. But if you coax the llama a little, he

Cover your llama's head and legs with fly wipe to discourage mosquitoes and biting flies.

should quickly learn that he can gently rub the fly off on the back of your shoulder as you hike along.

A collapsible bucket may already be on your camping equipment list. Some llamas may not be used to drinking from moving streams. My llama Coyote always had to explore the creek for just the right pool of water, smelling just so and not moving too fast. If he doesn't find it, he won't drink, even when he's thirsty. I offer all the llamas water from the bucket when we are in camp, both in the morning and in the evening.

To supplement the llama's browsing, I bring along a Ziploc bag of "llama granola", a mixture of processed alfalfa pellets and C.O.B. (corn, oats and barley, also processed to prevent spreading seeds).

Hand-held scales that will measure loads of up to fifty pounds may be purchased at sporting goods or hardware stores that carry fishing equipment. It is very important to make sure that your loads are balanced within two pounds. I find it handy to pack picket stakes and Ziploc bags of llama granola last, as a way of adding the extra pound or two to match up bag weights. I use a German-made scale that weighs accurately year after year, sold through Mt. Sopris Llamas.

You'll want to take along a brush to clean up your llama before saddling him for your day's hike. Small twigs and pine needles can work their way down into his wool and possibly cause saddle sores. A quick grooming of the area where the saddle fits him will help prevent unnecessary injuries.

Bungie cords and duct tape are two of those things like Velcro and Fastex buckles - you wonder how you made do before they came along. Bungie cords can lash down a top load. Duct tape is handy for quick repairs of bags or tents; I've even used it to wrap an injured llama's foot so that he was able to hike out. To have some duct tape handy when I need it, I wrap a long length around my Nalgene water bottle, in addition to carrying a small roll in with my other pack gear.

A length of nylon cord finds many different uses. It can be especially useful for repairs, putting up tarps, and hanging food containers out of the reach of bears.

Bells for free-grazing llamas

Many packers, including myself, allow some of their llamas to graze off the picket stake in camp. In this case the picket line is attached to the halter, however the stake is removed. I do this to disperse the animal's impact and allow thinner llamas a bit more to eat. I always have more llamas picketed than loose.

Bells are a good idea if you are going to allow any llamas to graze off their picket stakes. If a llama should wander out of sight it's comforting to hear him through the trees, and easier to find him as well.

The axiom of free grazing is *know your animals*. Don't leave a llama unsupervised the first time you let him graze off the picket. Don't go off and leave him loose if you're headed on a day hike, even a short one, unless you're sure he will be there when you return. Do not allow him to graze loose at all if you are camped right next to the trail. A string of pack horses and mules might come along and have a rather strong reaction to a loose llama wandering over to say hello! It can be quite a problem, and cause serious injury. I suppose there could even be legal implications.

Banjo was one llama I picketed for many seasons. Even though he was very herd bound - that is, he didn't like to be out of sight of his buddies on the trail - once in camp, he loved to explore.

I had noticed this trait the spring before I started to pack him. I took a group of llamas up into our hilly and partly wooded sixty-acre back pasture. The new grass was green and tender; when I turned them loose, the llamas started grazing immediately. But after a few minutes, while the other llamas were still grazing eagerly, Bandit began wandering over the knoll to investigate what was on the other side.

So when I began packing with him, I picketed him. I didn't think he would leave the group on purpose, but his curiosity might take him too far.

My suspicions were confirmed on a trip during his first summer of packing. He was picketed in a meadow, but when his stake pulled loose during the night, he went exploring. In the morning, I found him several hundred yards from camp, where his picket line had tangled in some small trees. He was as glad to see me as I to see him; when we rejoined the other llamas, his pleasure was obvious.

These days he's been with me for more than ten seasons, and I routinely let him graze dragging a picket line without being staked.

He always comes immediately to the sound of rustling plastic, in fact woe be to any hiker who takes a dip into their own "gorp" bag in Banjo's proximity as he will quickly seek them out and request a nibble (he loves nuts and raisins). He also has learned that, on buggy evenings, taking a position just downwind of a smoky fire provides a haven from the mosquitoes. Many's the time he's joined our evening campfire circle, where he kushes downwind, chews his cud and seems to enjoy the group's revelry.

Another word to the wise: be sure to catch any loose llamas before catching the ones on a picket line. One summer my camp helper gathered up all the picketed llamas, tying them in camp for saddling. The two remaining llamas who were loose saw what was going on and promptly decided that going back down the trail towards the truck was preferable to doing packing chores that day. Young Raphael's sturdy legs got a good workout as he followed the llamas seven miles down the trail before catching them, brought them back to camp, packed up their loads, and then hiked another seven miles to our campsite for that evening.

Chapter Seven
TRAINING YOUR PACK LLAMA

M ost of the llamas I have trained have amazed me with their ability to quickly learn packing tasks. No doubt it's the result of thousands of years of ancestral experience. Certainly anyone who has trained horses or mules will be impressed with how quickly many llamas learn to lead and accept a pack.

But keep in mind that a well-trained llama is the result of the successful collaboration between animal and human. If you want a llama that willingly lets you catch, halter, lead, and pack with him, you must give him considerate and consistent handling.

If you choose to train your own pack llama, make a concerted effort to do so with thought and patience. If you decide you don't want to tackle the task, buy a trained llama. Even if your llama is already trained to lead, to load in a trailer, and to accept a pack when you buy him, there are still things for the two of you to learn together.

In Appendix Four you will find a selection of books and videotapes that cover llama training. And Appendix Five lists several people who can teach you to teach your llamas. You may want to examine one or more of their books or videos. Or you may attend a clinic in order to understand more clearly the training techniques involved in teaching llamas basic obedience skills and in teaching them to pack.

I've been working with llamas since 1984 and have trained dozens of packers. I've learned a lot from my own experiences, and I feel indebted to other trainers who have shared their knowledge with the llama community, especially Bobra Goldsmith and Marty McGee. My methods today are a mosaic built from my own experience and what I've learned from others. As you gain experience in handling your llama, you will develop your own favorite methods too.

General guidelines

The most important training tools cannot be purchased from a llama supply catalog. Patience, relaxation and flexibility will take you a lot further in your training efforts than anything else. Schedule your training at a time when you have absolutely no other commitments or deadlines. Stay relaxed and don't feel that it's necessary for your llama to achieve any specific goals during your lesson. Aim for them, sure, but go only as far as feels right for that day. Be willing to alter your method to allow your llama to succeed.

Llama owners quickly learn that each animal is a distinct individual and will act and react in his or her own way. One llama will go through the training program in the blink of an eye, the next will have a hard time with certain steps. In time you'll recognize when your llama is bored or confused or too preoccupied with getting back to the herd to pay attention to you. Then it will be up to you to alter the program to fit the individual llama's needs.

Keep your initial training sessions short. At first, limit them to fifteen to twenty minutes. Several short sessions in one day can be more effective than one long, drawn-out lesson. Make it fun for your llama to participate. Don't be reluctant to use food rewards. And, if you do, give them sometimes just for the llama showing up, not as a bribe. Using food is not cheating if they learn; it's winning for both of you.

If you have more than one llama, remove the others from the corral or pasture where you will be doing the training during your initial sessions. They don't need to be out of sight; you just don't want them in your way, distracting your pupil during his lessons. Later, you may chose to leave them in, and, especially in the case of a young or nervous llama, having one or more of his buddies around can help him to relax and pay attention to you.

Llamas learn through repetition. A smart llama will learn a task after doing it three or four times. After he has mastered following you over the fallen logs and through a stream, only an occasional reminder may be necessary. Don't bore him by endless repetitions of a lesson. If you keep his interest keen, he'll be more agreeable and willing.

Be consistent and your llama will learn to trust you. By using a small pen for your early lessons, and utilizing the catching procedure outlined later in this chapter you can begin to create a positive, consistent pattern in your handling.

Any training session should end on a positive note. Even if the llama didn't manage to jump into the truck on his own, go back and repeat something he does know. Praise him for it before rewarding him by turning him loose. Keep in mind that letting him go is a reward. If he thinks he was turned loose because he balked, then he will remember to balk in the future. He won't be doing it from an ornery streak, but simply because he learned that it worked.

Don't force new lessons at every session. Make some sessions very relaxed. Do something your llama knows. Let him succeed, then take him for a walk.

The more time you spend with your llama, the more comfortable the two of you will be with each other, and the more easily you will pick up each other's cues. That extra time will certainly pay off out in the backcountry, on those days when weather or trail conditions put a strain on time and temper.

If you start out with more than one llama, or as you add more later, you will notice the individual differences of the animals. One will follow you right into the trailer the first time, but his pasture buddy may need to examine the floor, sides, and roof of this strange structure before he feels confident enough to step inside.

Punishing llamas

There will be times when your llama's ill behavior may seem to require punishment. Before you react with anger if he kicks or spits on you, analyze his motivation. Was he reacting out of fear or pain? At most, a strong vocal reproach is the best punishment for a situation when you believe the behavior was motivated be fear - kicking being the most common situation. Avoid being caught up in an "argument." Try to analyze the situation and determine how you can do what you need to do without causing the llama to feel threatened.

If you think your llama being willful in the face of your instruction, then a sharp tug on the lead combined with a sharp vocal reprimand may be in order. Llamas are stoic and will tolerate a lot of pain without learning anything from it, so hitting them is rarely effective. The best way to avoid punishment is interacting with your llama in a way that makes them feel safe and giving them positive reinforcement for good behavior. Soothing vocal praise, release on a tight lead, a handful of grain, and turning out after a good lesson are all forms of positive reinforcement.

Catching and haltering

The simplest way to catch a llama is to begin by herding him into a small corral, stall, or catch pen. Walk behind him with outstretched arms, encourage him to move in the direction of the catch pen, and tell him, "In." A fifteen-foot length of one and a half inch PVC pipe is a useful arm extender when you are herding. If your feeding area is in the enclosure, just throwing fresh flake of hay or rattling the grain bucket, especially if you do this at feeding time, may bring him in.

A length of PVC pipe can help out with herding tasks.

Once he's inside the pen, slowly walk up to him and place your lead rope over his back. Holding on to the other end of the rope, gently maneuver your way around the front of the llama and pick up the first end of the rope from his back. Now you have "caught" your llama. By not forcing him into a corner where he feels "trapped", and allowing him to stand or move while you put the rope around his neck, you can gain a bit of his trust.

Give him the command "stand" and slowly approach his side. If he walks away from you, give a firm pull on the rope and bring him back to a standing position. Once he's standing, repeat the "stand" command again. At the outset, it's best to use the command when he's doing the behavior you want him to learn.

Release pressure on the lead immediately whenever the llama is moving in the direction you desire. Llamas will learn to lean against steady pressure, so use a tug and release on the line to ask for movement.

If he places his head over the fence in order to avoid haltering, use the rope around his neck to reposition him back inside the corral.

The higher the rope is on the neck, the more effective are your signals. While it may seem faster to get the halter on while he's "immobilized" over the fence rail, you do not want teach him to accept that as part of your haltering routine. Take a little more time at the beginning to have him in the pen with you; it will make haltering simpler for both of you in the long run.

When he is standing still next to you, slide the rope up his neck to just below his head. Unless you spend additional time desensitizing your llama's face, you should touch it as little as possible as you place the halter over his nose. Hold the halter well open, guide it over his face gently, and use care in bringing the strap up behind his ears. I personally prefer to desensitize my llama's head, making haltering, as well as putting on fly repellent in the back country, easier. I use many of the techniques taught in T.T.E.A.M. training methods,

Picking up the draped end of the lead rope: a non-threatening way to "catch" a llama.

and they have proven very helpful for me, especially when working with llamas that come to me with haltering difficulties.

Your movements should be firm but gentle. Llamas are sensitive to touch. If it's too light or tentative, it will tickle; if it's too hard, the llama will recoil. Soothing verbal praise can reassure him and let him know when he's behaving as you want him to. If he pushes backward violently and gets away, stay calm, start over again, and remember to breathe while you're haltering him. That may sound a bit silly, but if you are holding your breath, the llama will too, and it's much easier to relax and learn if everyone's breathing deeply.

Try to keep his initial contact with the halter gentle and pleasant. If he has had an unpleasant experience with halters before you bought him, it may take him a bit longer to come to trust you. Many llamas learn to put their heads into the halter in a very short time.

Hold the halter open, then gently guide it over his face.

The nose band of the halter is placed high above the nostrils, and the chin straps are adjusted to allow the llama room to comfortably chew his cud.

Make sure the halter fits your llama's head. If the nose band is too low, it can press on the soft part of his nose, blocking his breathing. The halter should fit just loosely enough that it doesn't rub him or put pressure on his nose or jaw when he chews his cud. Notice how far his jaws move, and how his halter fits, as he chews his cud. If you need to make adjustments in the chin straps or throat straps of the halter, remove it, adjust it, and then place it back on the llama, unless you have desensitized his head first. I strongly advise you do not purchase or use halters that have a "fixed size" nose band. You should be able to adjust the halter in this area in order to get a proper and comfortable fit for your llama.

If your llama resists being haltered by raising his head or by attempting to duck away, you can use grain or hay pellets to "feed him into the halter." You might need to spend more time desensitizing his head. You may also place your arm around his neck, though this will often cause him to resist more. Do not use force to hold his head or neck in place. You're not trying to overpower him but rather to prevent his evasive maneuvers while you slide the halter on.

When you remove the halter from your llama, simply reverse the procedure. Place the rope around his neck, holding on to both ends. Then unbuckle the halter and gently slide it off his head. Some llamas may try to pull away quickly at first; avoid letting the llama throw the halter off with a fling of his head. Take a breath or two after unbuckling, but before removing the halter. Once the halter is off, make him stand calmly until you release him completely.

Do remove the halter. It is dangerous to leave a halter on your llama in the field. He could get snagged and hung up in a fence. It's also much more comfortable for him to have it off.

Leading

Most likely a llama you purchase will lead after a fashion. If he is somewhat reluctant to follow, you might try having someone walk directly behind him on his first few leading lessons. Your helper can encourage his forward movement with a tap on the rear when he balks.

Use a verbal command such as "walk out" as you initiate your movement so he will eventually learn to respond to your voice and action rather than to a tug on the line. Short, firm tugs on the lead will be more effective than a steady pull in coaxing a llama to step out. Again, release the pressure as soon as he moves in the direction you want.

Your goal is to have your llama follow you willingly on a slack line. Reward his movements toward you with a slackening of the lead and a word of praise. Gradually you can build up to a brisk walking pace. It's easier to train a llama to walk with a loose lead than it is to train a dog to do the same thing. For safety, never wrap the rope around your hand or tie it to yourself.

If he should simply balk and lean back in goatlike fashion, you can try walking off to the side, at an angle, and giving short, coaxing tugs on the lead. This will put him off balance, forcing him to take a step or two. Reward him verbally and by taking pressure of the lead as soon as he steps forward.

If he balks by kneeling down, you want to startle him right back up. Usually if you take a quick step toward him and sharply say "Get up," he will. Or pulling to the side with the lead rope with the firm command "up" might work. I've also had success by lifting up on a recalcitrant llama's tail, firmly and carefully. This usually surprises him, causing him to rise to the occasion.

Sometimes you'll encounter a llama that is balky and doesn't walk out lightly on the lead. When this happens I use trick I learned from Marty McGee. One summer joined me on a pack trip and we took along young Cinco, a three-year-old gelding I had raised, just start-ing his first big summer on the trail. He was built like an athlete - sturdy, trim and muscular. Cinco had gone on a couple of overnight treks the previous summer, and seemed to take to the tasks with ease.

This next summer he was balky, not too responsive to the lead, and hesitating over obstacles. When he walked behind me on the trail there was a lot of pressure on the lead rope, though when walking behind another llama he kept up better.

At Marty's suggestion we tried a different approach. We fitted Cinco with a halter constructed with rings on the side where the strap that goes over the nose joins the cheek strap (sold by Zephyr Farm, listed in Appendix Seven). We clipped a lead with a lightweight snap to that ring on his left side, instead of to the ring under his jaw as is usual. The change in his responsiveness was immediate. He obviously felt the cues clearly and responded more willingly. An important part of making this work was making sure that the halter was properly adjusted. The nose band stayed high up on the his nose, not dropping down to restrict his nasal airway.

Later that summer Cinco completed a thirty-mile trek and performed like a new llama. I used the alternate lead connecting point, though after that trip I was able to return the snap to the usual position under his jaw.

Tying up your llama

Always use a quick release knot to tie your llama. It's simple, it's safe, and it's easy to get untied.

To make a quick release knot, first wrap the loose end of the lead rope around the post you are tying up to. Then use that loose end to

Quick release knot, step one

make a twist, laying it over the other end of the rope that's attached to the llama's halter. Be sure the loose end is on the top of your twist. Second, push the loose end under the lead and up through the twist.

Quick release knot, step two

The third step is to pull the loop firmly to make the knot. Pull on the halter end of the rope to snug the knot next to the post. If you failed to make the twist properly in the second step, your knot will come undone. On a properly tied knot, one pull on the loose end of the rope will release the knot.

Quick release knot, step three

Handling feet

Llamas' legs and feet are very sensitive. Their primary defense is flight, and their instinct tells them to protect their feet and legs. In addition, as male llamas fight for their position within the herd, they often bite their opponent's knees in an attempt to make him kneel in submission. For this reason it is quite easy to teach a llama to kneel down or "kush." They do so almost involuntarily in self-defense when you apply pressure to their lower legs.

This natural reaction can make it a real challenge for you to pick up, hold onto, and trim your llama's feet. His tendency is to pull away, even to kneel down. If you are patient and work with this knowledge, in a few lessons your llama will allow you to handle his feet.

Since I come from a horse-oriented background, it was important to me that my llamas would allow me to pick up their feet. I make this an early lesson in their training, and I learned a lot by trial and error on my first lessons. Now I mostly use two methods of picking up feet. The first involves tying the llama loosely in a small space: about four by eight feet works well. Having a board behind him to restrict his movement is ideal. If possible, use a container or another person to feed the llama his favorite food treat.

The initial idea is to get him to keep his leg down, not pull away or lie down. I begin by firmly stroking downward on his leg several times until he holds his foot still. Then I stroke down and firmly but gently take hold of his fetlock - the joint just above the foot - while I say, "Foot, please." I hold it as loosely as possible and let him pull it around as much as he wants. The more I move with him and don't restrain his movement, the quicker he seems to relax and let me hold his foot. Don't worry if he pulls it out of your hand, just calmly start over. Remember to stay calm and relaxed as much as possible.

Sometimes handling the rear feet is more difficult. Kicking is more common. I stand close to his hip, facing the rear, and I repeat the firm downward strokes until he keeps his leg in place. Then I pick up his foot with the same "Foot, please" request, making sure to move with him as much as possible.

If I have a very difficult llama, and some just plain don't want their feet picked up and will often lie down, I have had some success with using a length of flat nylon webbing, one and a half inches wide, to make a foot loop. Using a slip knot, I make a loop big enough to go over the foot and then tighten it when I get it around the ankle. You'll have to devise your own method of getting it into position. Sometimes I can maneuver the loop into position on the ground and tap the llamas' foot into the loop, other times I have to get hold of the foot just long enough to get the loop over it. After allowing the llama to stomp the foot a few times with light contact on the webbing, I increase to steady upward pressure, raising the foot off the ground. I immediately let him have the foot back, then repeat the lift. Your llama must learn to stand balanced on three feet for this procedure, so be patient. Many llamas that have trouble letting you hold their foot with your hand are more willing to let you hold it with the webbing while you trim the nails.

It may take several short lessons before your llama calmly allows you to pick up his feet. With a difficult llama, I might simply hold his foot briefly for a lesson or two before I actually trim a toenail. It's obviously not the llama's favorite thing, so when he's learning this I don't do it every time I catch him. Keep in mind that this lesson is most unnatural for the llama. His instinct tells him to protect his legs. Don't punish him for kicking. He's most likely doing it out of self defense, not aggression.

This lesson requires the most time and patience of any I teach my llamas, but it makes an incredible difference if I need to doctor a llama's foot on the trail. It also comes in handy when I teach them to

As you pick up a front foot, hold it loosely, move with your llama, and don't restrain his movements.

load into a high vehicle. Often, my placing one foot up on the bumper will give them the message to step up and in. And it makes toenail trimming a routine chore instead of a dreaded ordeal. The key elements are to let him move his foot at first, don't try to do it by force, take lots of time, and give him a reward. Remember when you're trimming llamas' toenails that they are softer and easier to trim after a good rain.

This is one lesson that needs periodic repetition. Don't be surprised when, after time, he picks his feet up for you himself when you say, "Foot, please."

Kushing

You may choose to teach your llama to kush. The word "kush" comes from camel handlers - camels are distant relatives of llamas - and describes the act of kneeling into a sitting position, with all four feet tucked underneath the body. Kushing can be helpful if you are transporting a llama in a vehicle. It can also be used for putting packs on a llama, making the task easier for one person.

Kushing is not essential behavior for a llama to learn. If you do plan to teach him, then I advise doing so after he leads, loads, and allows you to pick up his feet. If you teach kushing before foot handling, he may sit down as you reach for a foot, thinking you are asking him to kush.

To teach kushing, lower the llama's head near the ground and tap on his front knees. This will usually cause him to kneel. Pressure on his back legs will make him sit all the way down. Once he sits, allow him to raise his head to an upright position. Praise him. Say "Up!" the moment he starts to rise if he does so before you ask him to get up.

Loading in a vehicle

Training a llama to step up into a trailer or vehicle can be one of your earliest lessons. It is usually easy and rewarding. Noted llama trainer Bobra Goldsmith starts by teaching the llama to step or jump over a log. From going up and over a log to going up and into a vehicle is a progression which llamas seem to learn quickly.

I begin by teaching my llamas to load in a trailer, and then proceed to teaching them to load into my pickup, which is considerably higher. As you approach your trailer, the llama may want to look a while at this dark space you're asking him to enter. Let him have a look inside. You should enter the trailer first and then ask the llama to come "up" or "in" while you give short tugs on the line. Try not to stand him too close to the edge of the vehicle where he will continually bump his knee as he attempts to raise it. He might think he is unable to get in.

Give him enough time to understand what you're asking. Sometimes it's helpful to count to 20 while your llama has a chance to let the whole idea sink in. Should he resist your best coaxing efforts, I've found that, if he's a llama whose feet can be handled placing one of his feet on the edge of the trailer or doorway will show him how high it really is. He will often follow that foot on in. It doesn't hurt to offer him a reward of hay pellets or grain, once he has walked in on his own. Repeat the loading procedure three or four times, and he should have it down pat.

Remember, if you physically pull your llama into the trailer he will not have learned the task. He must be participating in the process for learning to take place.

This loading ramp can be adjusted to three different levels for training llamas to load into the bed of a truck.

After a llama loads easily in a trailer or low vehicle, you can train him to jump up into the back of a truck with stock racks or side panels. I usually teach this lesson in two steps.

I begin with a ramp set up approximately half as high as the truck bed. I park the truck flush to the ramp, to minimize any gap between the two where a llama's foot could get caught. A stiff saddle pad can safely help to bridge a small gap, so long as it's placed in a way that it won't slip. A bit of non-skid carpet can be useful, too.

Gentle coaxing, little tugs on the lead, and a food reward usually have the llama stepping up and into the truck in one lesson.

When he is quite confident and adept at entering the pickup via the ramp, I teach him to jump up and in from the ground. The biggest challenge will be to keep him from moving off to the side while you're up in the truck. You may want to try backing up to the barn door or to a narrow gate. A human helper, if one is available, can prevent the llama from wandering off to the side of the truck. As ever, patience and food rewards are helpful.

At my ranch, I've constructed a loading chute with an adjustable ramp that fits in three positions: at truck bed level, halfway down, and flat on the ground. It has been very useful in teaching llamas to load into my pickup. The sides of the chute give the llama nowhere to go but up and into the truck.

When you are in the pickup bed and the llama is on the ground, stand a little to the side of where you want him to jump; don't tower over him, which could intimidate him. Make sure that the truck bed is not slippery - have it lined with rubber matting or carpet - and make sure that it's dry, so the llama will not lose his footing and injure himself jumping in.

Remember, if you transport your llama in an open trailer or truck, you should tie him to prevent him from jumping out. (Llamas have done this.) See the discussion in the chapter on transporting him tied. It wouldn't do any harm to practice tying him up a time or two during a training session.

Llamas can quickly learn to negotiate fallen logs.

Negotiating obstacles

After your llama has learned to enter a vehicle, it is a natural progression to ask him to follow you in negotiating other obstacles such as fallen logs, brush, low branches, and streams. You may not have all of these available at home, but you can improvise. The basic idea is that the llama learns to trust that wherever you ask him to go, he will be safe.

If your llama has no experience in walking through running water, he may try to cross small streams in one giant leap. This can be dangerous, especially if he's loaded with bulky packs. Begin early in his training to make him step into a stream and walk through. If possible, pick a watercourse with a firm bank and shallow flow for early training. Many llamas dislike mud, and they may not be eager to try deep water at first. Wear shoes that you can get wet; it's easier if you set the example.

No streams nearby? You may want to try training him to walk through an inflatable wading pool filled with water. It can be challenging, but also fun and useful. Even so, the first time he meets a creek is likely to result in an impromptu lesson.

You should be aware that there's something about walking in water that often makes a llama want to defecate. It's best if your llama doesn't pollute the water, so keep walking briskly and be prepared to give a yank on the lead rope if your llama starts positioning himself for a potty stop.

For your lesson in negotiating obstacles, allow the llama to understand what you're asking, and put as much variety as you can into the types of obstacles you present. If you have an older, trained llama, have him perform the task you are trying to teach while your student is watching. Llamas learn a lot by example.

Introducing pack equipment

After you and your packing companion have become acquainted, you will want to introduce him to the pack saddle and bags. Even a yearling can learn what it feels like to have cinches around his belly and a saddle with empty panniers on his back. Remember to avoid putting weighted packs on young llamas. They're still growing and aren't ready for heavier loads until they're over two years old.

Through previous handling and grooming, your llama should have learned to accept being touched all over his back and even under his belly. Firm strokes of your flat hand on his back, sides, and belly, will make him accustomed to your touch. Your goal is for him to stand calmly while you touch him along these areas. If he moves away, try to keep your hand flat on him until he stands still. Then you may remove it.

I used to train my llama to accept a pack by introducing the saddle to the llama while he was tied to the fence, but now I begin the saddling lesson in a catch pen no larger than 12' by 12', and have as tools a bath towel, a length of flat webbing eight to ten feet long, and some feed pellets or grain, whatever he likes.

I begin by holding the llama on a loose lead and showing him the towel. If he seems overly nervous, I sprinkle a few pellets on the towel and offer him a bite. If he's able to eat some pellets off the towel, he's ready for the next step, which is to put the towel on his back and let him walk around the pen. Then I position the towel so that it covers his rump, allow him to move some, then reposition it so that it hangs off his side, hopefully dropping off after a few steps. The idea is to allow him to feel safe with the towel or anything dropping off his back.

When he seems comfortable with this, the next step is to simulate cinches. Repositioning the towel on the llama's back, I drop the length of webbing over his far side just behind his withers, and either reach under his belly or use a stick or other tool to pick up the webbing. I lift both ends of the webbing, applying firm pressure under the llama's

Let your llama examine the saddle blanket before you place it on his back.

Working in a catch pen, place the blanket on the llama's side so that it will fall as he walks.

belly. If he wants to walk around the catch pen at any point, I let him at first, but he should learn to stand for this before I move on.

When he's accepted pressure under his belly, I angle the pressure so that he feels it from the side, and then down from the top. Finally, I tie the webbing using a quick release knot over his back and lead him with the "cinch" in place. This lesson usually goes quickly and seems to increase the speed with which a trainee will accept the saddle and cinches.

The next step is to introduce the saddle, following the same progression as with the towel. Present the saddle to him slowly, letting him sniff it and look it over before you place it on his back. If he seems afraid, use the pellets again, on the saddle. When you lay it over his back, be sure that your cinches are lying on top of the saddle, not hanging down of the far side where they could bump his legs and spook him.

As a horse person, it is most natural for me to saddle my llama from his left side. However, I believe that llamas benefit by learning to be saddled from either side, allowing them to become more accustomed to you working wherever you chose.

I have two methods of bringing cinches up under the llama as I'm teaching him to accept saddling. If the llama is not too tall, I place one hand over his back, sliding down his opposite side, pressing the cinch against that side and on under his belly as far as I can comfortable reach. With my other hand, I reach under on my side to bring it up. This way I don't bump his legs with the cinch. Be careful to make sure you don't get knocked off balance if the llama jumps away while you're leaning over him. If you have spent some time desensitizing his flanks and belly before beginning to saddle him for the first time, this should go quite smoothly.

If the llama is too tall or you're too short for that method, you can have a helper on the opposite side pass the cinch under to you. If no one is around to help, try fastening baling twine or a lead rope to the cinch ring, laying the twine or rope on the ground under the llama, taking care not to get it tangled in his legs, and then picking it up on your side and fastening the cinch.

Don't let the llama's wool become tangled as you fasten the cinch. Cinches may fasten with Velcro, Fastex buckles, or latigo knots. Place one hand flat against his side, palm out, underneath the strap or buckle as you fasten it. Then keep the wool clear while you tighten the cinch.

For the llama's first saddling lessons, you don't need to tighten the cinch as much as you would if you were heading up the trail with a full load. Make it snug enough to hold the saddle in place while still allowing you room to place a couple of fingers underneath.

If your llama is taking all this with aplomb, you may choose to go ahead and fasten the back cinch as well. If he acts skittish and unsure, remove the back cinch from the saddle. Save that lesson for next time, after he's had a chance to get used to the front cinch.

When you do use the back cinch, make sure that it fits well in front of the llama's penis. Good saddle systems will provide some way of attaching the two cinches under the llama, and allow for adjustment of the distance between them. If your cinches do not have this you can use a short cord to attach the back cinch to the front cinch.

Go ahead and take him for a walk now. Depending on how he's acting, you may want to brace yourself as you leave the catch pen. Some llamas react to the sensation of the cinch by trying a few bucks around the corral. This isn't common, but it happens now and then.

I have not had this experience often since I expanded the first lesson to include the introductory towel and webbing steps. Before then, when I introduced the saddle to a closely tied llama, I had a few llamas that bucked the first time they untied after saddling. In those cases I simply held onto the lead rope and let the llama jump around the corral. Soon he would be walking with the saddle on as if he'd always done it, however I enjoy having a way to do it now without creating such a stressful event.

Now lead your llama over an obstacle, or trot him up the drive. At some point stop and pat the saddle to remind him that it's there. In no time at all he should accept it like a second skin.

When introducing the panniers go back to the catch pen and use the same sequence. Let your llama see and smell the panniers, like you did with the towel and then the saddle. The bags should be empty for this lesson. Rustle them around a little as you put them on. He'll need to get used to the sounds they make.

With panniers in place, take him for a walk again, stopping to rustle them or to adjust the straps. He may walk on "tiptoes" a little at first,

Place a hand behind the cinch ring as you tighten it, to prevent tangling the llama's wool.

and may jump off to the side when he rubs them against the barn unexpectedly, but very quickly he should get used to their presence on his back.

Carrying loads

When he's accepted the panniers, the next step is to load them with something light and bulky. Sleeping bags or pads work well. Now lead him around and let him get accustomed to having something attached to him that will bump into barns and trees if he's not attentive. He's going to have to learn that his width has approximately doubled. Make sure your cinches are snug - you don't want the saddle turning with its load if he jumps.

If at any point he does attempt to buck his load off, hang on tight, keep the lead short, and try to keep his head low while bringing him back to attention. Stay calm if you can; he's reacting out of fear, and you don't want to make him more afraid by shouting or getting upset.

Your back cinch should be fastened snugly, but with enough room to slide a few fingers underneath.

After he accepts the panniers with these light loads, you may start introducing weighted loads. Find tasks that your llama can do with his newly acquired skills. Let him lug firewood from the woodshed to the house - this will give him good practice in standing to be loaded and unloaded. Try letting him carry something that rattles when he walks. Be creative; there are lots of potential chores for him to do under the guise of training and conditioning.

Next, begin taking some longer walks with the llama carrying a moderate load. This will get you both into condition, and familiarize you with packing a well-balanced load that rides comfortably.

Stash a rain poncho in your pack bag and, at some point in the walk, take it out and put it on so your llama gets used to it flapping in the wind. Sometimes llamas are startled if you bend over suddenly.

You might want to simulate stopping to tie your shoe a few times until the llama you're training gets used to your actions.

I have to admit that training the sixty or so llamas that I've worked with to date has been incredibly simple.

I had only one that failed completely. Harley was three years old when I bought him, the first baby llama born on the farm of a couple who had never before raised livestock. He was basically spoiled and he didn't like other llamas, showing it clearly by spitting on the other llamas he hiked with. While he led well, and hopped right up into the truck, he balked at performing menial tasks.

No amount of retraining seemed to help. He had a permanent chip on his wooly shoulder. I tried loaning him to a friend, thinking perhaps Henry and I had a personality conflict. Mike brought Harley back in a very short time. Harley had sat down in the trail, spat on Mike's llama, and generally ruined Mike's weekend.

I found a useful home for Harley with a herd of sheep, where he manages to keep the coyotes out of the field. The rancher's grandchildren feed him carrots, and he's is quite content not to see another llama or go packing.

I learned from another llama I bought that you can't assume anything about a llama's prior training. Murphy arrived on my ranch as a mature gelding. I purchased him from a woman who raised milk goats. She had bought him as an oddity; she knew almost nothing about his life before she acquired him. Murphy enjoyed herding the young goats around, she said, but he often stood at the fence "with a faraway look in his eye."

She had a photograph of him with a pack on. "Aha, he must be experienced," I reasoned. So shortly after I brought him home, I saddled him up. Omitting the early training steps, I loaded his panniers with windfall apples, intending to haul them out to the back pasture for the deer.

Murphy accepted his load with large eyes and ears askew. As we moved out of the corral area, his pack bumped the corner of the shed. He erupted into a mass of motion. He managed to pull the lead rope from my hands - the first, and for many years the only, llama to accomplish this - and bounded across the pasture. The packs flipped over and back. That startled him even more. Up until that moment, I had no idea that a llama could move so fast. He jumped the creek. When he finally came to a halt, probably only about thirty seconds had gone by, but it seemed much longer.

His saddle was listing considerably to one side. I approached him slowly, with gentle words I hoped would reassure him. As I got close, he bolted again, but only a few steps this time. He was figuring things out. I took hold of the lead rope, and slowly lifted his packs off.

One buckle was broken, but otherwise the equipment was intact. Unfortunately, I couldn't say as much for the cargo.

I led Murphy back to the corral, where I readjusted his saddle. Then I placed his panniers (that now contained windfall applesauce) back on, and headed out again into the pasture. This time he was much less frightened. I was very relieved after I unloaded the apples and we finally arrived back at the barn.

I'm glad I had taken this first walk in the confines of my pasture. Photos of packed llamas can be deceiving.

Later, I wanted Murphy to carry my aluminum cook box, which rattles and is wider than most of my other loads. He was very wary at first, but he never repeated his spectacular run.

After this for years, Murphy has gone on to distinguish himself on the trail. He carried that cook box on one side and a full-size cooler on the other. It was a pleasure to see him consciously maneuvering his wide load around trees in narrow spots on the trail.

As you undertake their pack training, most llamas will quickly show you why their ancestors were an integral part of South American life for thousands of years, adapting to their loads with an innate intelligence and remarkable style.

Chapter Eight
BEFORE YOU GO

At some point in your life with llamas you'll venture out on your first packing excursion. Before you do, let's look at a few important things to consider prior to heading for the trailhead - most importantly conditioning your llama and planning your trip.

Conditioning your llama

Conditioning walks are a benefit to both you and the llama. They help firm up muscles that haven't been used much since last season, and they help toughen his feet after a winter on soft pasture.

Where I live, my llamas are still on snow in the early spring. The moisture causes their pads to be especially soft. Walks on pavement give them little trouble, but gravel can damage the soft pads, leaving them sore and looking like a kitchen sponge. Pretreatments of Tanni-Gel, a product used to toughen field trial dogs' pads, can help to dry and toughen your llama's pads. You should be able to find them at your local feed or pet store or through your vet.

Your walks may be around your neighborhood, or on a favorite trail close to home. Llamas make fine jogging companions too. Beware of busy streets: you wouldn't want a gawking driver to cause an accident, and many llamas are somewhat scared of traffic at first.

If at any time during your walks, your llama decides he's not having fun, starts to hum incessantly, or tries to lie down, don't turn back to the barn immediately. Try to figure out what's going on. Is he humming because his saddle is rubbing or his rear cinch has slipped back? Does he need a short breather after an uphill climb? Is he anxious about being separated from his pasture mates? If he just seems to be complaining about the hike, continue until he appears to relax or to accept the fact that you won't give in. Then you can stop for a rest or turn around and head home.

Don't expect your llama to get into condition for carrying a fully loaded pack by taking a couple of walks around the block without even a saddle. Load him up. Use firewood, plastic milk jugs filled with sand, or whatever you have around the house, and give him a chance to strengthen the muscles he'll be using on the trail.

Start with a moderate amount of weight - forty or fifty pounds for an adult, twenty or thirty pounds for a two or three year old - and take him out twice a week or more. Two to four miles would be a good distance to cover. If weather and your time permit, you can do this year round; it's especially valuable for the couple of months before your packing season. If possible, make your walks include both uphill and downhill terrain; this will condition all your llama's (and your own) muscles.

During your conditioning walks, let the llama become accustomed to you stopping to adjust the pack, or removing things from it, while he stands still. Rather than tying him up, hold the lead rope loosely while you fiddle with the straps of the saddle, or open a bag and fish around in its contents for something. This practice will pay off when the day comes along that you need your rain slicker in a hurry and you left it down in the bottom of the pack. Your wooly friend won't be dancing as fast as you're digging.

How much can a llama carry?

The amount of weight that a llama can carry comfortably and safely depends on several factors: the llama's age, his size, his condition, the distance to travel, and the type of terrain.

By the time a llama is two years old, he's ready to go on overnight pack trips. Remember, though, he's still a youngster. Even if he weighs three hundred pounds, he's still growing. You don't want to subject him to undue stresses while he's still growing.

Be sure to keep his load, including the weight of his pack saddle, under forty pounds. He will probably accept his burden very well initially, but remember, he's just a kid, and his stamina will probably be less than that of a seasoned pack llama. Young llamas are impressionable: you'll want to make his first trips fun, not stressful. Keep his load light, set an easy pace, and give him plenty of rest stops during his first season on the trail.

These two llamas met on the trail during their first backcountry outing. Scout, the dark llama, was a robust two year old who packed thirty pounds. The other llama, an adult, packed more for his owners.

An adult llama in good condition may carry a load equal to between a quarter and a third of his weight. But assess his condition carefully. Don't ask him to pack a hundred pounds uphill for ten miles on the first trip of the season, unless you've done a fantastic job of conditioning beforehand.

An overweight llama is carrying his extra pounds, and consequently can't carry as many for you. If your llama has been a pasture potato all winter, start out with short trips and a moderate load. Burn off his extra pounds while building up his muscles. You can refer to Chapter Two for more information on how to evaluate the body condition of your llama.

If your outing will be along relatively easy trails with minimal elevation changes, you can expect a conditioned llama to carry his full pack with ease. If you will be crossing high mountain passes or scrambling around in deep canyon country, you may want to lighten his load by ten or fifteen pounds to compensate for the extra exertion of the trip.

Before your trip, load up your panniers with all the items you plan to take. Weigh them and weigh your pack saddle. This will ensure that everything is within the llama's physical limits.

An ounce of prevention

Before a trip, be sure to trim your llama's toes if they need it. This will prevent torn nails, stumbling, and discomfort or possible lameness from walking with his foot in an abnormal position.

Let your llama experience as many of the potential trail situations as possible prior to leaving home. He should walk calmly through small streams and standing water. He shouldn't be stopped by low logs or ledges. Some llamas panic when they first feel brush on their legs or bellies, so you may want to walk your llama through brush and high grass until it no longer bothers him.

Llamas should have experience in being on a picket stake line before their first trips. Most llamas quickly figure out how to negotiate the rope, but some become alarmed when they get their legs tangled up. These animals may need several picketing lessons at home before you take them into the backcountry and stake them overnight. You can do this by staking them out somewhere at home, keeping an eye on them until you're sure they know the ropes. Don't picket them near rhododendron, yew, or any other toxic plants. Check Appendix Three for a list of some poisonous plants, and find out about any that are common in your area.

How far can they go?

You might think that as a commercial packer, I would own a string of hard-working, perfectly conditioned llamas. Actually my llamas lead the Life of Riley. Many of the guests on my trips are totally wiped out after five or six miles, and are eager to make camp and sit by the campfire, enjoying the scenery.

As a consequence, my llamas get rather used to short hikes. They know the five-mile campsite up Hurricane Creek that I often use, and are very vocal when we pass it by on longer trips.

For many years I did what a lot of commercial packers do, planned easier trips early in the season, and worked up to the longer, steeper trails later in the year. Now I start in May and take four or five llamas at a time in a string on a couple of loops around my back sixty acre pasture. That's at least an hour of walking up and down hill, over a few logs and across the stream twice. Then they are "dry lotted" for the rest of the day, kept in the corral with no feed until late afternoon. They relax, chew their cud and wait patiently for me to let them back into the lush pasture for the rest of the evening. When school lets out I hire a couple of high school kids to help so that all the string gets at least three outings a week, and they're well legged up for packing throughout the summer.

So the question of how far you can go is always relative to how well-conditioned you and your llamas are, as well as to the terrain, of course. A general rule of thumb is that conditioned, experienced llamas should be able to handle up to fifteen miles a day over moderate trails. I'm the first to emphasize that your llamas should be in good condition.

One summer I began to offer drop camp services to a campsite nine and a half miles up the Hurricane Creek trail in the Eagle Cap Wilderness Area of the Wallowa Mountains. For a drop camp, an outfitter packs up the clients' own gear, takes it and the clients to the spot, and comes back later to pick them up. I fully expected this trip to be an overnight job for me. I knew I could get the people dropped off the first day, but I wasn't sure how far back down the trail I could get before the llamas or I gave out.

On this particular day, I was to meet the two clients at a trailhead near my ranch at 8:30 AM. For this special task, I chose my two most willing and long-strided llamas. Murphy, age seven with three seasons trail experience, was the cornerstone of my existence as a commercial packer. Palouse was a robust three year old in his second season in the pack string.

As I went out to catch Murphy and Pal, I noticed that Lydia, one of my female llamas, was in intense labor. She would surely have her baby that morning. She wasn't due until the following week, but her pasture-mate had produced a baby girl the day before, and Lydia was not one to be left out of the action for long.

She didn't have the baby before I had to leave, so I put my assistant on red alert and I asked the vet to come by and check on Lydia later in the morning. Then I saddled Pal and Murphy, loaded them into the truck, and made it to the trailhead relatively on time.

My clients, a mother and son, were good hikers. We were five miles in by eleven o'clock, when we stopped for lunch. I unloaded and

On an early spring trip into Hells Canyon, Pal and Murphy carry gear for their hikers.

picketed the llamas in a nice grassy spot. I don't normally unload the llamas for lunch breaks, but this time I wanted to give them a good rest, considering the hike ahead. We took a full hour break for lunch before loading up and heading out again.

The remaining five and a half miles went along a well-graded trail with little elevation gain. The entire hike climbed less than 2300 feet in the nine and a half miles. With several more breaks for water and photos, we were at the campsite by three in the afternoon.

I had carried a backpack with my own camping gear along. About a mile short of the final campsite, I left it at an old miner's cabin. After I said good-bye to my clients, I led Murphy and Pal back to the cabin, unsaddled them, picketed them, and let them graze for about forty-five minutes while I soaked my feet in the creek.

Along about four o'clock I began to get really curious about the new baby llama at home. I wondered if maybe we could get home that night. I wouldn't find out sitting there.

I saddled up the boys, distributing the contents of my pack between them. Going up, they had each carried about eighty-five pounds. Now, with my gear, the pickets, extra feed, and the large first aid kit I carry on commercial trips, they were each loaded at just under thirty pounds.

Down the trail we went, as fast as I could walk. We didn't take any extended rest breaks, but when we came to places in the trail where the grass was very lush, I would stop and let them fill their mouths as full as they could. Then I'd start right out again. They figured that procedure out right away. I thought they were both remarkably willing to start out again, munching on their mouthfuls.

Seven miles later, at Slickrock Falls, I met a couple of people I knew. So the llamas and I took a five-minute break for some visiting. Then we continued down, with only the mini-munch pauses.

It was 7:30 p.m. when we finally arrived at the trailhead, after nineteen mile day. Until the last quarter-mile, neither llama had made a sound or given a tug on the line, but on that last stretch they hummed frequently. They knew as well as I did that the truck was just a few minutes away.

I was amazed that we had done it. Llamas really can go almost twenty miles in a day, and do it well.

I attribute this accomplishment to several factors. First, both Murphy and Palouse were in very good physical condition, as the trip took place in July during a packing season that had begun in early June. Second, they were not loaded to their maximum capacity; at that time Murphy regularly carried one hundred pounds and Palouse at least eighty-five. Third, they had quality rest stops, at lunch and at the miner's cabin. Fourth, they are both outstanding animals with a lot of heart. I feel fortunate that they are in my pack string.

Since that trip, I have made the same journey in one day with other llamas, for drop camps. So don't sell your critters short if you want to try a more challenging trip. Make sure they're in condition, keep their loads a little lighter than you might on an easier trip, give them plenty of rest and refueling stops, and see what they can do.

Back at the ranch that day, Lydia had had a beautiful baby boy. The vet arrived just as the cria's head was emerging. This vet was fresh out of school and not really sure of normal procedure concerning llama births. He and my ranch helper, who was witnessing her first llama birth as well, haltered Lydia and dragged her to the barn - she was most reluctant to go. There he assisted in delivering the cria, basically easing it out as Lydia pushed. When I got the bill, the various charges were listed: "Farm call, $___ , selenium and tetanus shot, $___ , pull llama, $___" as in pulling a calf which is a common procedure with cattle. When I went down to the clinic to pay the bill I couldn't resist kidding the vet by asking him if I was being charged for the delivery of the baby llama or for pulling Lydia into the barn.

Route planning

At some point, you and your llama will be ready for your first extended outing. You may decide to choose an easy four- to six-mile round-trip hike as a test run. Some llamas, especially the younger ones, will find that plenty of challenge for a first trip, even if they are in good condition.

If you are fortunate enough to live near a national forest or wilderness area, you may already know a few places where you'd like to take your new packing partners. If not, or if you're planning a trip to a new area, then you'll need to do some research.

Many bookstores and libraries carry a selection of trail guides listing a number of hikes in popular parks and forests. These contain valuable information about access to the area, trail conditions, and facilities at the trailhead. In addition, outdoor magazines often feature articles on interesting areas to explore. Certainly other people who pack with llamas would be happy to tell you about places they have enjoyed visiting with their animals.

Once you've chosen a spot to visit, purchase a good map showing the area in detail. All National Parks and National Forests publish maps listing campgrounds and trailhead facilities. Some publish topographic maps, showing the elevation contours, while others focus more on roads and facilities.

It is best to have a topographic map of the area you intend to visit. If the National Park or Forest Service map isn't topographic, you can purchase U.S. Geological Survey quadrangles for that area. Appendix Four includes an address to write to for a list of U.S.G.S. topographic maps.

The U.S.G.S. quadrangles are printed in fairly large scale; you may need more than one to cover the area you will be visiting. They show forested and treeless areas, and some trails, roads, and springs. These are very useful features when you're selecting camping areas, and will give you a better idea of the terrain you'll be crossing.

The contour intervals on topographic maps mark a specific distance of elevation; intervals of fifty, eighty, and one hundred feet are common. By counting the number of intervals along your proposed route, you can determine the amount of elevation gain or loss.

The contour lines also give you other clues about visual aspects of the area. When the lines are very close together, they indicate that the terrain is extremely steep. When the lines are far apart, you can expect to find more level ground. In addition, contour lines will form a V when they cross a stream. This V will always point upstream.

Time spent studying maps is never wasted.

By using topographic maps to plan your trip, you'll be able to determine if you'll be climbing steeply to reach your destination or if you'll have an easy amble along a ridge line. The maps will also help you to judge more accurately how long it will take you to get to camp.

When you plan your trip, consider that every five hundred feet of elevation gain is approximately equal to another trail mile in terms of the travel time and amount of energy expended. This means that if it's four miles by trail to a lake that is two thousand feet higher than your starting point, the hike into the lake would be comparable to traveling eight miles on the level. Unfortunately, you can't make up the difference in elevation loss. It requires a lot of energy to hold the body back as you hike downhill, and a mile downhill is still a mile.

When you purchase a map, note the date it was printed. Many older maps may show trails that no longer exist, and they may omit newer trails or facilities.

Design your route so that you'll camp near a good water source, in an area with adequate feed for the llamas. For overnight trips, plan not to hike too far your first day. You should allow extra time for travel to the trailhead and all the adjustments that come with the first day out.

Young llamas, and unseasoned older ones, will enjoy the experience more if you take it easy on their first few outings. Plan a relaxed pace with regular rest stops - be prepared to enjoy the new sights and sounds of a leisurely trip as much as your llamas will!

Planning a trip on public lands

Just about every time we take an extended hike with our llamas, for a full day or for a week, we end up traveling on "public" lands.

Every member of the party enjoys an occasional rest stop.

National parks, forests and monuments, state parks, and lands administered by the Bureau of Land Management (B.L.M.) all fall into this category and are the most commonly visited areas. As responsible visitors we must be aware of any rules and regulations that would apply to our visit, especially since we will be accompanied by our llama hiking companions. On public lands recreation is only one use, and there may be restrictions on recreational use in consideration of other uses and management concerns.

It would be nice if there was one set of rules governing all areas for us as hikers and our llamas as our packing partners, and this is not the case. The diversity of the natural resources and management objectives on our public lands dictates a broad spectrum of rules and regulations. It's really important that we, as llama packers, be at least somewhat familiar with the system and how to work within it. Try to keep in mind that we're still the new "special interest user group" on the block, and in some areas our presence is still a little tenuous. The less friction we create by trying to ignore some regulation we might not agree with, the less problems we'll have in the future. You'd better believe that agency personnel really notice and appreciate it when we work with them, and they will remember it if some "llama people" ignore the rules.

So, let's say you've heard about this wonderful lake in a park or on forest lands from some other llama friends and now you want to go there for a picnic lunch or a weekend fishing trip. You find it on the map, you drive to the trailhead and you hike in. Great. There's lots of room to turn your truck around at the trailhead, the trail is clearly marked, and there's lots of grass for your llamas to eat near the lake. There's even plenty of room to picnic or camp and only a few other visitors. Wow, what a great trip.

So, fueled by this great experience, you find another likely looking lake on another map on a different national forest and you decide to make another trip with your llamas. Only this time you find it's a really rough road into the start of the hike, you encounter lots of logging truck traffic, and there's only a wide spot in the road for parking. The trail was last maintained at least five years ago, if that, and there was a recent timber sale that denuded the hillsides making the trip in to your destination less than scenic. To top it off the lake is very swampy and the meadow where you hoped to camp is a mosquito convention center. It could be worse. You could have arrived to find a big sign at the trailhead that prohibits any pack stock. But how would you have known?

The first guideline to trip planning is contact the office of the agency that administers the area where you want to visit. Tell them what you are planning and ask them if there are any regulations pertaining to your visit. Ask them how to obtain a map of the area, and if they have any suggestions for making the most of your visit. Even if you've been going to the same lake in the same wilderness area for years it's really a good idea to contact the administrative office. Regulations change. There may be new developments concerning road access or, especially in the intermountain west, forest fire damage. This can cost you a lot of time and headaches later, should you discover that the route you planned is subject to heavy horse use, blocked by snow, or hasn't been cleared since a big windstorm made the trail impassable. One phone call can save you a spoiled vacation.

If nothing else, by making this call you have done two really positive things - one for you and one for llamas in general. You have given yourself some peace of mind that you're less likely to have any unpleasant surprises, and you have alerted the agency that a responsible llama packer is using their public lands.

You may also plan a brief stop at the local ranger district office on your way to the trailhead. This is highly recommended if you haven't yet called the office to check on local conditions. Some areas require a backcountry travel permit, usually free, and this is a good time to get one. They often have an updated local weather report which is always good information for the backcountry visitor. The bottom line is you should either call or stop by the office before you go.

It's finally time to hit the trail and put some miles under those padded and Vibram-soled feet. The trip ahead of you will complete your llama's training, and reward you greatly for the time and energy you have spent up to now.

Chapter Nine
HITTING THE TRAIL

You're about to venture out on a full-fledged llama trek. Whether it's an overnight hike of a few miles or two weeks exploring a wilderness area, you and your llama will gain important trail experience that can't be gained in your own back yard. If your preference is day hiking, perhaps you are setting out on an all-day picnic hike with a few friends, carrying all kinds of luxuries.

If you have to drive for many hours to reach the trailhead, your llamas will be stiff after the ride. It will help to unload them for a brief walk once or twice during the trip. You may also want to camp the first night at or near the trailhead, to allow them a rest before they go to work. At any rate, be sure to keep your first day's hike easy, and allow the llamas to walk the kinks out.

Packing up

At the trailhead, tie your llama securely on a short lead, to your truck, a tree, or a hitching rail if one is available. With your slicker brush, give him a quick grooming to get rid of any twigs or other debris that may cause discomfort under his saddle.

Put the saddle on now, tightening the cinches snugly. Then pack up your gear, giving him a chance to relax and let out any air he may have sucked in while you were cinching him up.

As you pack the panniers, place items with sharp edges away from the side of the bag that will be right next to the llama. You want that side to ride as comfortably as possible.

When you organize gear to load in your panniers, remember that you will want the weight to be as even as possible on each side. You can top-pack lightweight, bulky items, such as sleeping bags, sleeping pads, tarps, or tents that weigh under ten pounds. Set top pack items aside at the start, but remember to figure their weight into the total the llama will carry, making sure that the top load is not more than twenty percent of your total.

Once you have balanced the bags as evenly as you can by picking them up, weigh them with your hand scale. Rearrange the contents, if necessary, to bring the bags within two pounds of each other.

Weigh your bags to make sure the loads are balanced to within two pounds.

Loading panniers on the llama is easiest with two people.

Now check your llama's cinches and tighten them if they're loose. Then attach the load on one side to the pack saddle and continue supporting that side until the bag on the opposite side is loaded. This procedure is most easily accomplished with by people working together.

If you're packing alone you can load one side, then the other, and then make necessary adjustments if your saddle has tipped.

When attaching the panniers to the saddle, snug them up close to the point of attachment and make sure the bag's compression straps are cinched up tight, keeping the load compact. Remember that the panniers should not hang down below your llama's belly or interfere with his front leg movement. If the panniers flop around as the llama walks, he'll tire much faster, an important reason to avoid bulky, off balance loads. I highly endorse pack systems that have a way of lashing down the bottom of the panniers, either with a strap running under the llama's belly or by attachments to the cinches. Both the Flaming Star and Mt. Sopris Packs offer this feature.

When both panniers are in place, securely attach your top pack items with straps or bungie cords. What you're packing and the type of saddle you use will determine the best way to arrange the loads. Many saddle systems have straps or bags for top packing. If yours doesn't, you can strap the load down with short bungie cords. A duffel bag can be used to hold sleeping bags, sleeping pads, and other light weight items.

Remember not to place heavy items directly over the llama's spine, and make sure that none of the top-packed items will poke or rub the llama's flexible neck as he turns this way and that during the day.

Finally your llama is packed and you've scanned the area around your vehicle to make sure you haven't forgotten anything. You shoulder your own lightweight day pack and begin your journey. For the first half mile or so, keep a close eye on the llama's load to make sure it's riding well and not shifting to one side or the other. Especially on your first few outings, you will no doubt need to make regular adjustments as you learn how best to lash down your top pack and how different straps and attachments fit your animal.

If your pack system allows you to raise or lower the pack bags on the llama's side by lengthening the sling straps, you can compensate to a limited degree if you discover that one bag is slightly heavier than the other. By lowering the lighter bag, thereby lowering its center of gravity, you will help even out the distribution of the load on the animal. You may get by without having to repack your gear.

You can also add a rock or two to the light side. If you've done much backpacking, it may go against the grain to add an item you don't need. Just don't think about that bottle of wine you left sitting on the kitchen table because it was too heavy! It's important enough to the llama's well-being to have his pack even, that he'd rather have the rock.

Nearly every time that I take Cupcake into the backcountry, he reminds me of our early pack trips together. He was one of my first llamas, and quickly became the leader of the string for our training outings.

At the trailhead, I would painstakingly load up, learning what worked by trial and error. I would often need to make little adjustments in loads, or to rearrange the order of the pack string, after traveling only a short distance.

I was nervous at first, but after hiking a while with everything riding in place and all the llamas content, I would begin to relax. I'd look around with delight at the mountains and the llamas.

Then Cupcake would sneeze - loudly. I would jump in surprise, and skip a heartbeat or two.

He still sneezes during the first mile of a hike. I often hear a little exclamation of surprise from the person leading him that day, and I chuckle in remembrance of those early trips.

Stringing them out

Leading more than one llama at a time is easy - they tend to follow one another willingly - but there are special considerations. It's a good idea to practice this at home first. Some llamas are more touchy about having another llama at their rear, and you may have to alter their order in the string to accommodate their preferences. Often,

Hiking with a string of llamas requires attention, and sometimes fast thinking.

they need only a short time to adjust. If they are pasture mates, you can expect little problem.

Fasten the trailing llama to the pack saddle of the leading llama. Use a knot or connection that is secure, yet may be quickly released if your llamas get in trouble. In many cases when you need to un-hook them quickly, you'll be dealing with taut leads. For example, your llamas may be wrapped different ways around the same tree, so make sure you can undo the connection quickly and easily without requiring slack in the rope.

I use a large rubber band when connecting llamas in a string, a trick I learned from llama and horse packer friend Betsy Adamson of Redding, California. The rubber band will stretch, compensating for slow starts or unexpected stops, but will only break under extreme pressure, and then is easily re-tied or replaced. Sometimes younger, balky llamas continually break the rubber band, so I'll tie them to the saddle of the leading llama with a quick release knot until they learn to walk up at the pace of the leader.

Llamas tend to hit the end of the lead rather forcefully at times, so training your llamas to walk out on a voice command will certainly help that problem. There will still be times when young llamas choose to walk around the opposite side of a tree, quickly bringing things to an abrupt halt.

Your string of llamas will soon let you know in what order they will travel most comfortably. Some animals will want to walk faster and try to pass the llama in front of them. Others are more content to be within the pack; they may not really like being first. And you may find other llamas who prefer being last, in the caboose position, since nobody is on their tail that way.

You'll discover the optimum order by trial and error. Don't be surprised if the same llama who wants to be in the back of the string going up the trail decides he'd rather be in front coming back out to the trailhead.

A rubber band can be used to connect two llamas safely. Consult the diagram in Appendix One for more information.

Train your string to walk single file.

It took me a few trips with llama Levi to discover that he liked to be second from the end of the string. If he was farther up in the line, he constantly looked back to check on the others. If he was last, he got nervous and tried to walk in front of the llama he's supposed to be following. Levi's retired now, but Ranger, one I raised here on the ranch, has developed this same trait.

Often you can deal with a slow llama by positioning him at the back of the string, where he will speed up to keep from being left behind. These considerations are also pertinent if each llama is being led by a person.

Train your pack string to stay on the trail and to follow in single file. If they're not in a line, they're much more likely to get tangled up with each other and with obstacles. Besides, their impact on the environment is less if they are all on the trail than if some of them are hither and yon on either side of it. So watch how they go, especially in open meadows. You can direct the sideways-straying llama, "Line out!" while with your hand you motion him back in place. You may have to step back and place him in line a time or two, but in my experience llamas learn this quickly.

If you have two or more llamas strung together, pay special attention to how they are traveling. Look back often to check on their loads, and take special care when negotiating obstacles. Individual

Levi is connected to the llama in front with a correct amount of lead rope. If this rope were any longer, either llama could step through it, becoming seriously tangled.

llamas following a person are not particularly prone to cutting across switchbacks, but when they are in a pack string, short-cutting, which contributes to trail erosion, is more likely. Here again, "Line out!" can be effective.

Trail behavior

As a rule, llamas are very calm on the trail. When startled, they'll take a defensive hop to one side, then stop to reassess the situation. Their only natural predator in South America is the mountain lion, an animal that often hunts from rock outcroppings. So if something appears above them on a hillside, llamas will jump back instinctively. But even then, they will not customarily bolt in blind terror.

I hiked with llamas for about eleven years before I had "a run-away" one summer. Two year old llama Jim Dandy was on his first overnight trip. He'd been a bit nervous the first day, but made the five mile hike in to camp with about thirty pounds in his pack in good form. The next day we were leading the group of hikers on the way out and doing fine. Then, as we entered a large meadow, he suddenly bolted. The next llama packer in line behind us, Victor, said he noticed that Jimmy had kicked at something just before he took off, and we later concluded that he'd very likely been stung by a bee or horse fly.

At any rate, as he flew by me along side the trail, I instinctively knew that holding on to the rope was not an option. As he raced across the meadow I removed my day pack and started walking briskly after him. As he ran, one pack bag came loose and the other tipped the saddle, causing the second bag to hang down under his belly. A classic "wreck" was unfolding.

About two hundred yards from where he started, Jimmy turned and came racing back toward our small group. He was bellowing in fear now as the pack struck his legs, and I was suddenly confronted with a large llama, scared out of his wits, coming straight toward me at a dead run. Thankfully he veered when he reached me, I grabbed the lead rope for a brief moment and said firmly "Jimmy, whoa", giving the lead a tug before letting go again. He stopped a few yards past the group of llamas and people, where he stood still, panting heavily. I walked up to him quietly and took hold of his lead rope. Then I released the cinches on the saddle, removed the one pannier, gathered up the second and began re-saddling, putting everything back in place.

It's a rather anticlimactic ending, but Jimmy stood quietly for the whole procedure (as he was catching his breath, I'm sure) and then hiked out without further incident. He's been a solid packer ever since and, to me, this is an illustration of how most llamas seem to recover from "traumatic" experiences with minimal ill effects.

Hiking along the trail you will often notice your llama walking along the trail's outer edge. You may not like this if there is a steep drop on that side, however most likely, the llama is trying to look around you to see the trail ahead. Llamas follow one another readily, but they don't always trust us two-leggeds. If this concerns you, try walking a little farther in front of your llama so he can see more of the trail as he goes along.

Remember that when going down steep sections of trail, llamas have difficulty walking slowly. They carry approximately sixty percent of their weight on the front half of their body. Add the weight of the packs to that, and you can see why they like to keep moving down the hill. The added weight and the momentum create a lot of stress on the front legs. Be sure to give the llamas room to choose their own ways down steep sections, and give them a good rest stop at the bottom of a long decline in the trail.

At times as you hike, your llama may follow you quite closely or even try to pass you on the trail, like the tailgating of an impatient driver. This is most common when you're on your way back to the trailhead.

Sometimes I think llamas have two speeds: in and out. Two miles an hour is a good heading-in pace. That's fine. Their packs are heavy, and who wants to rush? Coming back out is another matter; the pace can really pick up.

If you find a llama stepping on your heels and crowding you on the trail, there are several things you can do to discourage his tailgating. Hold up your hand at eye level, and sharply say, "Back!" You may have to repeat this command at intervals to get your point across. Remember, though, as with any one-word command you give a llama, use it just once each time you use it. If you say, "Back, back, back," in quick succession, then the llama will think that the command is three words (or not get it at all).

Some packers will twirl the end of the lead rope to discourage an animal that wants to pass. I've also carried a light tree branch, and use it to touch the llama's chest or front legs if he continually gets too close. One or more of these methods should work for you.

At some point on your hike, you will find yourself brought to an abrupt halt. Your llama has stopped to relieve himself. Unlike horses, llamas have to stand still during their potty stop. It can take them a while, so stretch and relax. Cupcake has a favorite spot on a switchback trail up to Slickrock Falls where he never fails to stop and lighten his load. I make a point of kicking the pellets off the trail, but every spring he still finds that spot. Often llamas will step slightly off the trail to deposit their pellets of dung. If you are leading more than one llama, you will no doubt witness a chain reaction as the whole string gets into the act.

Speaking of abrupt stops, be careful about how you stop. If you don't give your llama some verbal or physical cue that you are going to stop, he is likely to keep walking - perhaps into you.

As you go down rocky trails, give your llama a slack lead and let him pick his own way.

Don't let your llama slow you up by grazing as you travel. He should learn to hike while you're hiking and to graze, if he wants to, only when you pause.

Balking on the trail

Lots of people ask me what to do about their llama that balks, lies down or just plain quits on the trail. Often this is a younger or novice packer, though occasionally the problem llama is one that's had one or more hiking seasons. Not always an easy question, it usually takes a little investigation to discover an answer.

If the situation involves a young llama in his first season on the trail, quite often the problem is simply that the llama is not ready for what he's being asked to do. Is the llama in condition, is the load heavier than he's used to, or is the trail too demanding for his level of experience? I don't mean to imply that llamas are wimps, quite the opposite. But I've learned that if a novice pack llama is started out gradually, with light loads on relatively easy trails, taking regular rest stops, he has a chance to learn and accept his task without having to fight discomfort - physical or mental.

The first few times on the trail a novice packer is usually busy checking out all the new sights and smells. Some of them are strange and a little scary. Add to that the recent ride to the trailhead. Unless your llama has been a frequent trailer traveler he may be suffering a little bit of "road shock", and now he's in a strange place with a pack on. Together, all these things can weaken a new packer's level of confidence.

So, how can you make the first trips easier and lessen the chance of a problem on the trail? Step one is to make sure your llama is accustomed to his pack and to a load similar in size and weight to the one he's carrying. Give him experience in the truck or trailer. Haul him here and there a few times, especially if he seems to be a nervous rider. Make sure you plan an easy hike the first time or two. And, when possible, take a seasoned packer along to provide experience and companionship.

Two novice packers out together on a strange trail for the first time can really play off each other's insecurities. It may be hard for either one to take the initiative and walk right out as a leader. If this is your situation and you don't have an experienced llama to lead the way, take a gentle hike and plan to keep the pace slow. You may have to alternate leaders - not all llamas like the responsibility of walking first into the unknown. It's also possible that either one will do fine in front. If this is the case, I encourage you to switch leaders occasionally to encourage their independence and flexibility.

An experienced pack llama is a very valuable training aid. After a novice llama has gone through his initial packing lesson, I bring an older llama into the picture to provide a bit of confidence. With both llamas in the same corral I go through all the procedures, from brushing to saddling, on the older llama first. The novice watches what I do with the pro, then he's next. It often seems to lower his anxiety level. And, if I have a trainee that's especially skittish about some part of the training, I'll even try placing him between two seasoned packers.

Out on the trail, the older llama will not be nervous and soon the youngster accepts that, if he just follows this guy, he'll stay out of trouble. You play a role in making this work by keeping an eye out for potential problems. If you come to a stream or a boggy area, find a safe, easy crossing. Perhaps you'll come to an area with several fallen logs to cross. If you have the two llamas strung together be sure that the trainee can make it over the log without the leading llama jerking him across. Go slowly through the obstacle and perhaps lengthen the lead between the two llamas, or take them across separately.

If the packer that's balking is older, with more trail miles under his cinch, you'll want to ask some of the same questions and perhaps look a little deeper into the situation. Is he in shape? Certainly an out of condition llama will not be able to give you a peak performance. Conditioning is essential whenever you ask an animal to carry a fully loaded pack all day long. If your packer is out of shape you may not only have problems with his performance but you run the risk of his sustaining an injury along the way. You won't want to pack out the load of a llama that's lame, so don't neglect your early season training hikes, or plan an easy trip with a light load.

If you're having trouble with a conditioned llama perhaps there are problems with your gear. Is the saddle fitting properly? If your llama is uncomfortable from a pack saddle that is digging into his back, he may decide it's not worth it and go on strike. Be sure to thoroughly evaluate your pack saddle by the methods described in Chapter Six. Remember there should be good spinal clearance with any type of pack saddle. Most saddle pads will not correct a poorly fitting saddle; eventually the llama will become sore.

Finally, a llama that just doesn't want to get up and go may be ill. If you're well into a trip and he's been performing fine up until now, consider the possibility that he's eaten something poisonous. Do you know the toxic plants in the region where you're packing? Also, make sure all vaccinations and wormings are done several weeks prior to a pack trip. Know the signs of heat stress as well as hypothermia. These problems can affect llamas as well as people.

Encountering obstacles

Crossing streams is something your llama should have learned before you ventured into the backcountry. If not, be sure to take time on your first trips and make him *walk* through streams during crossings. Do not let him leap across in one big bound. This is not safe for you, nor for him. He could be injured if he lands on rocks or uneven ground.

Avoid letting him stand still in the stream, or he may take a potty stop. There is something about cold water on llamas' feet that triggers this response. Once one llama starts, any others that are behind may follow his example. If you are going to offer him a drink, do so at the edge of the stream, before crossing, then walk quickly through.

Swift, high water can be dangerous for your pack llama. Do your best to avoid it, even if it means a long detour. If you have no choice but to cross, you may want to unpack your llama, ferry the loads across yourself, and lead him across unburdened, making sure he's on the downstream side of you as you cross. While llamas are reported to be able to swim, if your llama has never swum, this is not a good situation for him to figure out that he can. And I doubt that he could with a full load.

Murphy takes a drink. It's best to offer your llama a drink before entering the stream, diminishing the chances of an unwanted potty stop.

Obstacles such as fallen trees may cause you to detour, but usually you can find your way past them easily enough. If you are traveling on a seldom-used or remote forest trail, you may want to take along a small ax or Sven saw in case you find a fallen tree blocking your way. You may be able to pass safely by simply cutting off a few branches.

Take care in boggy sections of the trail. Many llamas do not like to have their feet sucked under the mud. They may leap and lunge in their effort to get through. Give your llama a loose lead and stay out of his way as much as possible when crossing bogs. Better yet, find a safer, alternate route.

Train llamas to step, not jump over logs.

If you find the trail covered with snow, don't despair. Your llamas come with built-in crampons; their toenails help to give them excellent footing on compacted snow. If the snow is very soft and over their knees, however, they may break through and have difficulty walking very far. If you run into any problems, remember that it will be easier to cross snow fields early in the day, before the sun has a chance to soften the snow.

Weathering the storm

Both at home and in the mountains, llamas are extremely hardy creatures, able to put up with all kinds of weather conditions. You may be totally tent bound while it's raining cats and dogs, and your llamas will most likely be sitting down, calmly chewing their cuds. Even when their outer coat seems soaked, usually their inner wool insulates them, keeping them warm and dry.

You may wake up early on a chilly morning and see your llamas' backs covered with frost. This shows just how efficient that insulating layer is. It traps their body heat so well that the frost won't melt until the sun comes up.

Rain coupled with wind over a longer period of time can penetrate the llama's wool, however, and you may choose to bring your llamas in under trees for more shelter in these conditions. If that is not an option, you may use your pack's rain cover to fashion a "raincoat" for your llama. Mt. Sopris Llamas sells a pack rain cover that is specially adapted for this use.

Llamas' toenails give them excellent footing on compacted snow.

Lightning storms present a threat to both you and your llamas. If you get caught hiking in the open during a thunderstorm, head immediately for cover and lower ground. If your llamas are picketed in a high, open meadow and a storm blows in, bring them up closer to cover so that they won't be the tallest thing to attract the lightning.

I've awakened more than one morning to find that a pleasant outing had turned into a winter wonderland. The first time was on a September trip into the high country. A storm blew in during the last night, and what I thought was rain beating against the tent all night turned out to be wet, icy snow. There was a couple of inches on the ground, and it was still falling. The llamas were visibly shivering as I brought them in for saddling. I brushed as much of the sleet out of their coats as I could, saddled them up, and headed home.

You'll need to be prepared to deal with more extremes in weather when you take spring and fall trips. Rivers may be swollen with runoff early in the year, and snowstorms are more likely to surprise you in the spring or fall than in the summer. Go prepared. Take along extra clothing for yourself and extra high energy feed for the llamas. They'll need it if the weather turns cold. And they will also need it if you go into areas where the grass has yet to green up in the spring or has been all used up by the end of the season.

Very hot weather

On the opposite end of the spectrum, really hot weather can be extremely debilitating to your llama. To prevent heat stress, you'll need to take it easy on very hot days. Don't attempt any rigorous hikes, allow plenty of rest stops, and make sure your llama has a chance to drink as much water as he wants at any stream crossings. Don't be alarmed if you see your llama stretched out lying in the sun, forsaking any nearby shade. It's very likely he's ventilating himself as he exposes the woolless areas under his belly and legs to the air.

On a May trip into Hells Canyon one year, we experienced a couple of ninety-degree days along the Snake River. At home the week before, we'd had snow flurries so the llamas weren't really used to the heat. Pal seemed to suffer the most - that surprised me, because he's a light-wooled white llama. I noticed him panting a lot along the trail, and we took several breaks for him and some of the other llamas to catch their breaths. In camp, after we unloaded and picketed the llamas in the meadow, Pal was the only one who still seemed to be breathing rapidly. I took him down to the creek to let him cool off by standing in the cold water. It seemed to help, and he finished the trip in fine shape.

On other summer trips I will occasionally have a llama show signs of overheating on an especially hot day. In this case I'll remove his pack and saddle during a break or lunch spot, and wait until he has recovered before moving on.

Pal's breath is labored after a hot, uphill climb. On this early-season trip, he was still out of shape. After a short break, he was ready to hike on.

Regular rest breaks will enhance the trip for you and your llamas.

Rest stops

Your early experiences will make a lasting impression on you and on your animals. Most likely, you'll be delighted to see how interested your llamas are in every little aspect of the journey. Don't rush them along the trail. Allow for small rest breaks every forty-five minutes to an hour on the first few trips. Let them learn what they can do. If they find it enjoyable, they'll retain their enthusiasm - and so will you. As your experience and conditioning build up, you may find that your rest breaks come less often and usually fit right in when you're thirsty or hungry or want to take a photo.

If you take a rest stop of ten minutes or more, tie or picket your llamas well off the trail so you won't have to move them if a horse party should come by. Llamas will often sit down and chew a bit of cud during a break. Or they may greedily munch on tree twigs and bark if they get little of these delicacies at home. Don't allow them to browse on very young trees which would be damaged by the nibbling.

Meeting horses on the trail

Most likely, you will be sharing the trail with other backcountry users, both hikers and riders. Many will be curious about your wooly companion. Some time spent answering their questions will go a long way toward furthering the llama's positive image.

You almost always hear horses before you see them. There's nothing very quiet about a horse party coming along the trail. This advance warning gives you a chance to make your best possible effort to assure a safe and pleasant encounter.

When I hear horses coming, I quickly look around to see if there's a convenient and safe place to get off to the side of the trail. I holler out a greeting, "Hi, hang on a minute and we'll get out of your way." Since I'm usually responsible for six to ten critters, that space off the trail is sometimes cramped. Many times a smaller group of horseback riders will go off to the side and holler back, "Come on through."

The rules of the road in the backcountry are the same as those at sea: the most maneuverable craft - or in this case, animal - gives way. The hiker should politely step aside for anyone with pack stock, and the llama packer should give as much clearance as possible to anyone traveling with horses, mules, or burros. If this means I must turn around and go back down the trail a half mile to a spot wide enough for the horses to pass, then that's what I do. I try to get at least ten yards off the trail.

I figure there are at least three things I know about horses. Number one is that they're big, lots bigger than llamas. Number two is that they are an integral part of a deeply cherished Western tradition of backcountry use. Number three is that they may never have seen a llama before, and the unexpected sight may give them the same kind of adrenaline rush you would experience if you turned a bend in the trail and saw a flying saucer parked off to the side.

Chances are good that the horses will not give you and your llamas a second glance. But a horse is a reactionary animal, not nearly as prone to reasoning things out as a llama is. I really work to avoid a strong negative reaction from the horses and mules that I meet. I do this by giving them lots of room, standing as far off the trail as possible - below it if that's an option. I address the riders in a calm and friendly tone. This helps to reassure their stock as well as maintain good will among the humans.

Most horse packers I meet are friendly and truly interested in my llamas. Many will stop so their animals can take a longer look. Some even ride a little closer, to let their horses and mules get more accustomed to the smell and appearance of my llamas. "How much do you pack on those things, anyway?" is the most common question I hear.

Doesn't sound so difficult, does it? Well, there was an afternoon a few summers back when a young llama, third in a string of three, took a misstep and went down off the trail in a terribly steep section. It was a heart-stopping moment, and then quite a job to get him back up and repacked. Fortunately, he was neither injured nor terribly upset by his mishap. The importance of having quick release connections on llamas strung together was brought home to me that day. I had looped the rope over both crossbars of the pack saddle, and we had a difficult time getting enough slack to get it undone.

We were finally on our way again. There were five people and eight llamas heading up the trail. Horses appeared ahead of us, coming downhill. The hiker leading a llama at the back of my line chose a real dandy spot to go off the trail, straight up a side hill. The other hikers followed him up with their llamas, so I did too. While I was getting quite concerned about our footing, the horse packer was marveling at how wonderful and amazing our llamas were, waltzing up that steep bank! He was really impressed.

I can't say it was a pleasant moment for me, but I bet the llamas got some good publicity from that packer down at the local tavern that night!

Well trained llamas tackle a variety of trail conditions with ease .

Chapter Ten
IN CAMP

At the end of the day's hike, you and your llama will come around a bend in the trail and you'll spot the perfect camp site nestled up next to the trees, not too far from the stream, and with a great view of the surrounding peaks. It's time to unload and relax. It will take only a few extra minutes to get your llama settled into camp.

Remove your llama's pack first, and then choose an open area in which to picket him. Try to find a spot that's visible from your central camp area so you can keep an eye on him. Make sure it's some distance from the trail and well away from streams or springs. Llamas seem to choose the dampest spots for their dung piles, and you don't want to contaminate the drinking water.

It is a good idea to examine your llama thoroughly before placing him on his picket line. After you unsaddle him, feel along his back to see if he has any tender spots or places where the hair has been matted. Look closely, as a llama's wool can hide a small saddle sore. Be sure to look underneath him, where the cinches fit, also. He can get sores there too. The llama first aid chapter discusses what to do if you find a sore. But normally everything will be fine. By taking this time to inspect your llama, you will know for certain that the pack saddle fits him comfortably and safely.

Choose a picket site where he won't get his line tangled up in small logs or trees. Remember, he may gorge himself on the variety of new plants within his reach, especially if all he gets at home is hay. Don't picket him near potentially poisonous plants or tender young trees that he might destroy. When staking out two or more llamas, place them far enough apart that they won't get their picket lines tangled.

If you are camped more than one night in any area, you should move your llama to a fresh grazing spot morning and evening. Moving his picket will minimize impact on the campsite and allow him fresh feed. Remember to scatter all the dung piles before leaving camp, and to generally leave things better than you found them.

You may want to offer your llama a drink of water from a bucket if he hasn't been drinking from streams on the way in or if it's really hot. Don't be concerned if he isn't interested right away, but try again shortly after you've fed him his granola, and again in the morning. The amount of water that a llama drinks varies from one llama to. Although llamas are related to camels, they cannot go for extended periods without water.

At the end of the day's hike, Cupcake drinks from a collapsible bucket, and gear is laid across a downed log.

Don't forget to give your companions their reward. The llama's ration of llama granola will help replenish his energy for the next day's journey. Don't pour it out on the ground, where the small bits of grain will be difficult to pick up. Let him eat it out of the plastic bag, use a paper plate, or feed it by hand.

You should get in the habit of hanging up your pack saddles and extra llama gear whenever possible. Little gnawing creatures have a way of finding leather straps and sweaty cinches if they are left within easy reach.

Free grazing

If you are camped some ways from the trail and from any horse parties, you may want to allow one or more of your llamas to graze off the picket stakes. This free gazing has lighter impact than confining a llama to one area. If you choose to do this, be sure you know your llama! Llamas are generally herd-oriented animals, but you wouldn't want to do this with a llama out for the first time, one you know wanders, or one that you can't catch easily with grain. You may leave the picket line attached and dragging behind the llama, making him easier to catch, but don't let anything dangle from the end that could get stuck on something and injure the animal if he starts running through the meadow. If you're traveling with just one llama, I don't recommend letting him graze off the picket.

One of my packers, Pardner, showed me the hard way that even the most herd-bound llama can leave the group under the wrong circumstances. As a three year old, Pard was not an enthusiastic packer and would have preferred to stay home with the females, doing his part to bring new little pack llamas into the world. I kept telling him that

Kristen feeds Banjo a bit of llama granola as a reward for the day's labors.

only the good packers got to make more packers, so he would have to prove himself on the trail.

He didn't like it but was giving it a go.

On a layover day in Hurricane Creek Meadow, I allowed Pardner to graze off his picket. He was wearing a bell, and his twenty-foot picket rope was trailing behind him. His brother Levi and Coyote were also loose; the rest of the llamas were secured.

Levi and Coyote were fast friends, and they were trustworthy. On this afternoon, they went exploring a little distance into the trees on the side of the meadow. Pardner got his rope tangled around a small tree, and could only see that they had disappeared. When I untangled him, he went off in search of them. A few minutes later, I looked up to see him disappearing down the trail that led out of the meadow and back to the truck.

As I trotted down the side of the meadow after Pard, Coyote and Levi came out of the bushes and looked intently after him. A group member herded them back to camp while I followed Pardner's direction.

I couldn't believe that he would really leave, so I kept looking off to the side of the trail, hoping he had stopped to graze. Then I approached the top of a hill and heard his bell - thank goodness he had one on - way ahead of me down the canyon. This convinced me that he was doing his best to catch up with Levi and Coyote.

I was hot on his trail, but it was another mile before I caught sight of him. I'd like to say that he heeded my plea to "whoa" but that was not the case. It was another three miles before I was able to grab hold of the end of his rope. Even then, it was no easy task to convince him that he should turn around and go back up the trail.

It started raining on our way back. A soft drizzle at first, it increased as we neared the upper end of the canyon. When Pard and I reached the meadow, the rest of the llamas were sitting down, chewing their cuds, and trying to ignore the rain. I let Pard go. I knew he didn't have the inclination or the energy to leave again.

I didn't hesitate to let Pardner graze off the picket after that incident. I just made sure that he could see the others, that all the loose llamas had bells on, and that I kept tabs on them to prevent their getting confused.

Layover days

Both people and llamas like layover days. This is the time that you can go fishing, explore, climb a mountain, or just relax. The llamas enjoy a day off from their packs, lounging in the meadow, nibbling an assortment of backcountry greens.

I like to give my llamas the day off on layover days, but many hikers will pack up their lunches in the panniers and take their llama along on their day hike. Toting such a light load is surely easier than a long day under a full load, and there's no reason why he can't munch along the way.

I've never had any problems leaving my llamas unattended while I've gone out day hiking, but I have heard stories of llamas getting loose and wandering off. If you take off for a day hike, make sure your llamas are securely picketed well away from the trail. When you return, offer them a drink of water and move their pickets to a fresh source of feed, and scatter any dung piles.

Lost llamas

I've been really lucky and have never had to deal with losing a llama in the backcountry. It happens, though, and before you go, you might give some thought to how you can prevent the problem. If you make sure your llamas will come to a bag of feed, you should have very little trouble catching one that gets loose. Be sure you picket any llama that you don't trust to stay close to camp. I don't advise anyone traveling with just one llama to let it graze off a picket. It also helps to put bells on your llamas, both loose and picketed. The sound of the bell will make it easier to find any llama that wanders off.

Llamas have been spooked in the night, pulled out their stakes, and disappeared for days. Other llamas have gotten loose and simply walked back to the trailhead. From the llamas' point of view, they weren't lost; they just checked out early, no doubt causing considerable worry to their owners.

If you do lose a llama, taking another llama along on your search party can help a lot. Their herd instinct is very strong. I know of one

A relaxing layover day is fun for everyone.

llama that got loose in a wilderness area during the summer, and evaded his owners for several weeks. Then, near the end of the summer after a couple of hard frosts, he found his way back to the trailhead on a day when two of his pasture mates were tied to a trailer, waiting for the searchers. He was calmly standing with them when the search party returned.

Other stories have not had such happy endings, so be sure that your picket stakes are in securely and that your llamas will come to a rustling bag of feed. I keep a small bit of llama granola in my day pack for emergencies, and it's been useful on more than one occasion.

Unwanted visitors

It takes just one bear experience to change the way you sleep in the wilderness.

It was three in the morning one July, a few years back, and our group was camped in one of my favorite spots - a long meadow ringed by spruce and subalpine fir in the upper reaches of Hurricane Creek. I woke up suddenly from a sound sleep with the distinct feeling that I'd heard a metallic sound, and then I definitely heard the sound of a llama calling in alarm. Both Kristen, my assistant, and I sat up at the same time, and without a word began to crawl out of our sleeping bags and put on our shoes.

As I left our tent I grabbed my flashlight and shone it out across our camping site, a small bench just above the meandering creek. The beam passed over the five other tents that were occupied by ten adventurous women who had hired me to be their fearless leader for a week in the Wallowas.

Thinking that the unusual sound had come from an area down the clearing, below my tent, I started looking in that direction. A wet smear was visible atop a large fallen log on the edge of the campsite near one of the tents. Then I directed the light to the llamas that were picketed nearby and I noticed that their attention was focused behind me, toward the camp kitchen area. At that moment I heard another crash, and I shone the light into the grove of spruce trees where our kitchen was located. There, caught in the beam of my flashlight was a furry-faced critter nimbly prying the lid off one of the plastic buckets that store our food supplies.

Now, I feel an admiration and a deep respect for bears in their natural environment, however my wilderness camp kitchen was not their natural environment.

"Grab some rocks, Kristin," I called. Then, "HEY YOU, outta there!" I pitched a few rocks into the kitchen, miraculously missing my stove and cook box, not to mention the bear. But I did get his attention.

A few voices from inside the tents asked what was going on. "We've got a bear in the kitchen," I responded. Several of the women came out to lend hands and voices to our bear shooing efforts.

Our verbal and granite barrage soon sent the bear ducking out through the trees behind the kitchen. Kristin and I went in to survey the damage. One food bucket rifled, a few emergency ration instant soup mixes gnawed on, and the cooler knocked over, but seemingly intact.

We carried all the food buckets, the cooler and the aluminum cook box into the middle of the campsite, covered them with a tarp, and put a few pots and pans on top of the pile. (I read about this tactic once in a story about camping in the Alaskan tundra where there are no trees to hang the food in.) We brought over two llamas and picketed them next to the pile, then quickly ducked back into our tents, shivering in the darkness of three a.m.

A short ten minutes after we went back to the warmth of our sleeping bags, I heard the sound I didn't want to hear - the llamas' alarm calls signaling that the bear had returned to the edge of camp. Without the burden of awakening from a deep sleep this time, Kristin and I were up in a flash. We pitched rocks and banged the pots (I'd read that, too somewhere). The bear scooted off into the darkness, out of our flashlight beams, only to return one more time a few minutes later. This time I got a good look at him walking across the lower meadow. He was a fairly large black bear with a plastic bag of trail mix in his mouth. He seemed to be on his way, content with his prize. I noticed a hint of dawn to the east and felt we'd seen the last of the bear for the night.

Now that the bear was gone I became acutely aware that the frost was settling into the meadow grass and I was clad in only a T-shirt and tennis shoes. Taking a moment to survey the star-filled sky I suddenly noticed a shimmering glow off to the north - the aurora borealis, not a common sight in these parts, and one I felt worth the bear experience.

In the morning we found a pilfered pack bag that had been hung in a small tree next to one of the tents. Our bear had neatly torn open the outer pocket in order to remove the bag of trail mix. Two inches higher and his claw would have snagged the zipper pull, saving me a repair job.

Now, I'd been hiking in the Eagle Cap Wilderness for more than nine summers. I had seen bear tracks, bear scat, and bear hair, but, until that night, I had never seen a whole bear.

Bears are hunted during certain times of the year in this area, and are commonly very wary of people. But somewhere down the line this fellow had learned that camps were good pickings. After the incident I felt a little sad, knowing his willingness to approach humans would probably lead to his ultimate demise at the hand of a hunter.

We camped in that spot several more times that summer with no sign of the bear. We heard a few stories from other campers who had encountered bears in that area; they seemed unusually plentiful that year. Kristin and I both slept a lot lighter for the rest of the season, and made special efforts to keep our camps clean and burn all our leftover food. We also picketed a llama near the kitchen for the rest of the summer

Some llama packers in Montana regularly picket a llama next to their tent at night, to act as a sentry should any bear approach camp. Bears seem to give llamas a wide berth, and that's fine with me and my llamas.

It's very important to practice good bear country camping techniques if you venture into areas that are known ursine haunts. I wouldn't rely only on llamas to guard your kitchen. Be sure to hang your food high and to keep your cooking area at least one hundred yards from your tent area. Don't cook or store any food in your tents. Don't leave any food or garbage near your campsite when you depart; burning it is better than burying it. You don't want bears to come to associate campers and campsites with a free lunch made up of your leftovers.

When you get home

If you have returned from an early season hike through brushy country, examine your llamas for ticks. The most likely areas to find them are under the belly and on the legs; see the chapter on llama first aid for tick prevention and remedies.

Check over your llamas for any signs of saddle sores before letting them go. Be sure to remove the halters from all your llamas as you turn them loose. Watch them move across the pasture and look for any signs of lameness that you might not have noticed on the trail.

The animals have worked hard; offer them a reward of grain or hay pellets. Don't be surprised if some llamas indulge in a vigorous roll in the dust wallow before attacking their bonuses.

Check your pack equipment for any signs of wear and tear. Take care of any needed repairs right away so you'll be ready for your next outing. You might also want to take a minute to think back on how the trip went. How might you make it better the next time? Did you need everything you took? Was there something you wished you had along? Were the llamas' loads too heavy or just about right? Did the animals perform as well as expected?

It is only through actual trail experience that you learn the most important lessons of packing with llamas. You may discover, as I did, that it can be one of the most rewarding experiences of a life-time.

Some musings on the low impact aspects of llamas

Are llamas the low impact pack animal we think they are? As I've worked with wilderness managers and talked with friends who are "hard core" backpackers it has been interesting to examine more closely the claims that we llama packers have made.

Llamas will usually indulge in a vigorous roll after a hard day on the trail.

As a volunteer for the International Llama Association I spent many years working with other dedicated packers to convince public lands managers that llamas deserve separate recognition from other pack stock primarily because of their lower impacts on the land. Studies conducted in the 1990's showed that when llamas are compared to horses, mules and even burros, there can be little question that padded feet do not destroy trail tread and compact soils in fragile environments as shod hooves will. It's an often overlooked fact, though, that when llamas are poorly managed in the backcountry, they can do substantial damage to plants, trees and water sources.

At lunch time and once they've arrived to camp, packers tie their animals to a handy tree for the break or to unload. The big problem with tying horses to trees is that they will paw and compact the soil around the base of the tree. Llamas will not do this but they will often begin to eagerly dine on the tree's bark. On older, established trees this will do little lasting damage if the llama is tied for a short time. However, on young trees and especially those that are used repeatedly at a specific campsite, a llama can have a bigger impact. Packers can limit the damage by making this opportunity as short as possible, and moving their llamas onto pickets soon after unloading.

Once in camp, the majority of llama packers picket their animals out on ten to twenty foot long lines attached to a swivel stake screwed into the ground. The llama is confined to this spot until moved and will quickly begin to nibble up the more savory morsels in his allotment. If any small trees are within his space they can be mortally damaged by not only the browsing, but also if the llama becomes wrapped around them. This is why care must be taken to picket llamas away from young trees.

If the llama's picket site is moved regularly (at lease twice a day when laying over or if feed is sparse) then grazing impact is kept to a minimum. But if it's a hot, buggy day llamas will have an overwhelming urge to take a dust bath, and will paw at the ground to construct a wallow. In high alpine meadows this can leave a lasting scar. As a remedy, they may be picketed close to an already bare patch of ground so they can follow their instincts without doing as much damage.

Somewhere inside his picket area the llama will choose to start a dung pile. If packers take a minute to kick the dung piles and spread out the pellets when they move the llama, then the site is fertilized. If this is not done, however, in dry or high elevation regions the piled dung will dry out rather than decompose, and it will actually inhibit plant growth beneath it. I have returned to campsites I use each year and have found barely decomposed pellet piles that were overlooked the previous year. The llamas usually choose that spot again and I have a "second chance" to spread it out when we leave.

Free grazing, or allowing a llama to wander loose, usually dragging a length of rope, has a lower impact in some ways. The llama is not restricted to a small area and can spread out his browsing and grazing. But in this situation there is still potential for major impact to small trees and to water sources. A llama will usually choose a damp spot to start his dung pile and packers are very familiar with the problem of their llamas wanting to stop in the middle of a stream crossing to defecate. Loose llamas in camp have the chance to walk right out into a stream and take their potty break. Obviously this will not do much for the water quality, and while it's true that wildlife and horses crossing streams do this quite often, we have the ability to manage our llamas and can take steps to avoid the problem. Some llamas are known offenders and the minute their feet hit the cold water they begin to go. These are not good candidates for free grazing near running water. Perhaps packing a pellet sample in (or along from the last camp) and providing them with the initiative to place their pile in the spot of your choosing would be a lower impact alternative.

Llama packing, both commercial and private, is opening the doors of the wilderness to many people who would otherwise never venture into the backcountry overnight, and is therefore affecting an overall increase in environmental impact. For this reason, we as llama packers have a special responsibility to practice low impact, no-trace camping skills.

A properly managed pack llama can leave little impact and actually allow campers to carry fuel for cooking (avoiding the need to burn wood), to pack in a substantial shovel to properly bury waste, and to easily pack out their own garbage as well as any they may find left behind by less mindful backcountry users. In this way llama packers can maintain the llama's environmentally positive image and protect the valuable natural resources in the areas they visit.

Low-impact camping guidelines

- First and foremost: pack out what you pack in. You may burn paper garbage if campfires are allowed in the area where you're camped; otherwise, carry out your trash when you leave.

- If fires are allowed in the area you visit, keep them as small as possible, extinguish them thoroughly, and remove all trace of their presence before you leave. Burn only dead and down wood for fires; for cooking, use stoves.

- Take care to dispose of human waste properly, in an eight-inch hole dug with a trowel or small shovel. Burn, bury, or pack out toilet paper.

- Don't use soaps or detergents in any stream or lake. Wash yourself, your dishes, and any clothing by using a container, and dispose of the waste water at least two hundred feet from any fresh water source in a "gray water" hole.

- Do not camp or allow your llamas to graze within two hundred feet of any lake or spring.

- Avoid prolonged stays in fragile alpine environments. Camp at lower elevations, and day-hike to these areas.

Chapter Eleven
THE BACKCOUNTRY KITCHEN

P acking with llamas has many advantages, and one of the best is that, with a little imagination and advance planning, backcountry meals can be carried to new heights, literally and figuratively!

Backpackers who count every ounce and leave behind fresh fruits and vegetables in favor of fruit leather, freeze-dried stew and instant oatmeal, drool at the delicacies dined on by llama packers. Instead of foil-packed lasagna, you can bring the real thing, prepared at home or from the freezer case of your favorite supermarket. Now you can delight in green salads for dinner, and a nice juicy melon for breakfast. Don't leave the fresh apples behind - your llamas may insist on the cores at lunch time. Hot whole grain cereal will warm you from head to toe on frosty mornings, and now you can enjoy it with fresh fruit and yogurt on top. You'll have to watch out, though, or before you know it you may be gaining weight on your pack trips instead of losing it.

As you think about how to enjoy this most delicious aspect of llama packing, consider the following suggestions as a basis for creating and executing your own backcountry culinary experience.

Hikers help themselves to a delicious lunch along the trail.

Menu planning

Eating well in the back country conjures up different images for different people. Some campers have a passion for concocting delectable Dutch oven dishes and elaborate meals from scratch over a wood fire. Others, myself included, like to keep meal preparation simple, while enjoying a variety of taste treats. Then there's the beans, bacon and cowboy coffee contingent who's entire camp cook kit is a plate, spoon, fry pan and can opener. Whatever your style, the basic methods of planning, organizing and packing food for your llama trek are very similar.

The keys to menu planning are simplicity and imagination. Think about your favorite stovetop meals, and how you can adapt them to camping conditions. Sauce for pasta can be made ahead with fresh ingredients, frozen at home, and then reheated in camp. Omelets are easy to prepare, and eggs will stay fresh in your cooler for several days. Look through your recipes and think about how they could adapt to back country travel. Keep an eye out for new dishes, and give them a trial run at home before you pack them up for a wilderness trip. Make sure your meals will be easy to prepare in camp. You never know when you'll need to cook in a rainstorm or arrive back at camp late and have to prepare a meal after dark.

Some commercially available devices are very handy. Many packers use a Seal-a-Meal® appliance to package all sorts of dishes from stews to pizza. You may even seal and freeze your favorite deli dish for later reheating in camp.

If you love good coffee, purchase a cold water extract device, and enjoy the convenience and great taste it offers without the constant mess of grounds and filters. You can get the cold water coffee gizmo at kitchen shops; one brand is Filtron, another is sold under the name "Coffee Toddy." It's a very nice way to do coffee at home, too.

If you enjoy wine with your meal, you may choose from the assortment of boxed wines at your local supermarket. The wine box bladders, once empty, make great camp water bags.

If haute cuisine is not really your idea of fun, then scan the supermarket shelves for easily prepared rice and pasta dishes that come in a box. With the addition of one or two fresh ingredients, you'll have an energy-packed meal. It may sound odd, but Stovetop Stuffing with a few almonds or mushrooms thrown in makes a great breakfast dish, along with Canadian bacon, and fresh or stewed fruit.

Trail lunches can be imaginative assortments of fresh and prepared items. Pita bread packs nicely, and you can fill it with all sorts of veggies, cheeses, and salads. Tropical dried fruits such as mango, papaya, and pineapple can add an exotic touch at lunch time. Pumpernickel or canned Boston brown bread spread with cream cheese is good fare on an energetic day. Big bran muffins served with cheddar cheese and fresh fruit are a hearty and wholesome lunch combination.

On my commercial trips, we occasionally have a last-day picnic lunch of all the odds and ends left over from the previous meals, along with nut bread, fruit, and cream cheese. On one of the trips, there was a guest from New York who worked for General Foods. She thoroughly enjoyed trying a variety of combinations of the assorted goodies, and admitted, "This is how new products are developed!"

So after you have an idea of what you'd like to eat during your outing, plan a menu for the entire trip, including every meal for each day. Remember that a hiking trip menu should include lots of complex carbohydrates for energy and minimize heavy proteins. Don't forget trail snacks, and plan on eating a little something every three hours or so. If you're counting on catching fish for dinner don't forget to take an emergency ration (dare I suggest freeze-dried lasagna or a can of beans?) just in case they're not biting.

Staying well hydrated is very important, so include some lightweight beverages such as Crystal Lite, herb teas as well as instant soup mixes. These will give you more incentive to keep drinking fluids.

Plan your menu so that you'll use the more perishable items early in the trip. Longer trips will be more challenging to prepare for than shorter ones. You'll want to use fresh food at the start and gradually work into your supply of dried and canned goods. Canned foods may also contain ingredients that will enhance some fresher item on your menu. Water chestnuts for a stir-fry? Picante sauce for enchiladas? Salmon or chicken for rice curry? Fruit topping for a last-night, no-bake cheesecake?

Food preparation at home

From your menu you'll have a shopping list and then what I call a "to do" list. I believe that the more food preparation you can take care of in the comfort of your own kitchen before the trip, the quicker and easier your backcountry meals will be. Grate cheese, chop sturdy veggies, freeze marinated meat, cook up a zesty pasta sauce, and then package these items securely in Ziploc bags or plastic containers. Repackage any pudding or sauce mixes along with dried milk if called for, and label them, including the amount of liquid you'll need to add and any other instructions.

Pack your fresh eggs by breaking them into a Nalgene bottle you can stow in your cooler. If you'll be making scrambled eggs, you can stir them up at home, pour them into a container, and freeze them for longer storage. If you don't stir them before freezing, the yolks take on a rubbery consistency, but the flavor is the same.

Now make a detailed packing list for your food. For example, if you're having oatmeal for breakfast write down oatmeal, salt (I put mine in the baggie with the oatmeal when I'm packing) yogurt or instant milk, and whatever you put on your oatmeal such as dried fruit, cinnamon, or butter. Be sure to include such things as the butter and syrup you'll want for your pancakes, as well as any spices that can add a savory touch to your meals. Many packers take along a Dial-a-Spice dispenser as a permanent part of their cooking gear

If you're calculating serving sizes from the information on a package of rice pilaf or pasta, for example, it's a good idea to add *at least* one extra "serving" for every two people. After all, you'll be feeding hearty back country appetites.

It also helps to make a detailed list for your camp kitchen gear, right down to the napkins, matches and any special utensils you might want such as a whisk.

A roll-up table is a wonderful luxury. Here it holds an aluminum cookbox, and creates an excellent serving area.

Of course, the real trick to making these lists work is to check them off as you pack, and then remember to keep the menu handy. More than once I've packed up everything and then left the menu at home on the counter. Luckily, we have a lot of the same meals every trip, so it wasn't too hard to figure it out when to eat what. If you really want to be organized, you can pack your food by meals or by days. In other words, all the nonperishables lunch items together or all the items for a specific day together.

Appendix Two includes some of my favorite recipes for pack trips. They are easy to prepare, they pack well, and all have been popular for several seasons on my commercial pack trips. There's homemade granola, lemon basil chicken, breakfast quiche, and a variety of other things, including some items for the sweet tooth. And see Appendix Four for my favorite packing cookbooks.

Packing the kitchen

If you're used to planning for backpacking trips where you had to carry everything, you'll need to readjust your thinking when deciding on kitchen gear. Coolers, cook boxes, and buckets can be used to enhance your camp kitchen. If you wish, you can take along more stoves, or a larger one.

Packing with llamas allows for quite a few luxuries, especially compared to backpacking. One luxury is the ability to take along a cooler, A "six pack" size cooler will work great for a weekend hike and, on longer trips you're limited only by the size of your panniers and the amount of weight you want to put on one side of your llama.

Coolers come in three styles - Styrofoam, plastic and soft sided, fiber-filled types. The Styrofoam ones are not too durable for continued use. Rigid plastic coolers come in lots of sizes, are durable, easy to clean and will make good containers for bottles or other garbage you may pack out from your trip. Soft sided coolers are lightweight, and can compress down to take up very little room after they're empty.

**Some packing friends and I sat down one day
in a glorious wilderness meadow and had a discussion
on how to make a cooler work to its best advantage.
Here are some of our ideas:**

- Freeze as many items as possible prior to the trip. Meats, sauces, butter, cheese, syrups, scrambled eggs and guacamole all freeze well,

- If you're using a small cooler and if it fits, put it in the freezer along with the frozen items, the night before your trip. Pack the other cooler items in just before you go.

- Protect delicate items from frozen items in the cooler. Lettuce and other vegetables may suffer frost bite if packed next to hard frozen items. Protect them with dish towels or place less delicate items in between.

- During the trip, open the cooler as little as possible. Especially on long trips it helps to pack first-day cold items together in a smaller, soft sided cooler bag, keeping your main cooler closed up until day two. Seal the second cooler with duct tape and wrap it in a space blanket for maximum cold storage-ability.

- Fill up the empty space in a cooler with a lightweight, insulating layer such as a spare pile vest or jacket. A cautionary note: Don't use spare clothing if your trip takes you into bear country. Take along a spare towel or improvise some other insulating layer that you won't be wearing or have in your tent later on.

- In camp keep your cooler in the shade, covered by a space blanket with the reflective side on the outside. On layover days look for a shady spot next to or in a cool stream. Weight down the cooler with rocks if you put it in the water. (If you're out early in the season, make sure this isn't a stream that will rise during the day as snow melts!)

- On longer trips two smaller coolers may work better than one large one. One can stay sealed with items that will be used later in the trip while you eat your way through the first one.

- "Blue Ice" or other ice substitutes are a waste of room and weight. If you do have extra room and weight, and feel the need for ice, then freeze some tap water in a plastic bottle and use it for drinking water after it melts. Use larger frozen food items as your "blue ice", and plan your menu so their use is spread out through the trip.

They may not protect more fragile items though, and I don't think they keep things cool as long as rigid coolers. They also come in different sizes and the smaller ones can be convenient for top packing picnic lunch items, allowing you to make lunch accessible without changing the weight in your panniers in the middle of the day's hike.

Many handy packers have constructed their own cook boxes out of wood or aluminum. Some of these are quite elaborate, with shelves, a place for a two-burner gas stove, and hooks for kitchen gadgets. Something of the sort is a must for the organized packer. At night, the boxes can be closed to keep out hungry critters. There are manufactured aluminum boxes available for sale in various outdoor catalogs.

If you're looking at one of these, be sure to keep the dimensions small so your llama doesn't need a two-lane trail to get to camp. Also keep in mind the weight of the box. You won't want to give up too many pounds to the container, or you won't be able to take along those extra goodies.

Many packers use square five-gallon plastic buckets to pack nonperishable foodstuffs. These buckets come originally filled with mayonnaise, mustard, and other such things. If you ask around at fast food restaurants, you should be able to locate some buckets. Two will usually fit in one average-sized pack bag. They prevent soft foods from being squashed, they keep out critters, and they make great little stools around camp.

You'll want to take along a good stove or two for your back country kitchen, and you have several options now that your llama will be carrying the weight. If you already have a good backpacking stove, you can start with it, but consider buying another one- or two-burner stove to expand your meal preparation options.

Kitchen items to take along

Utensils:
- Gas stove and fuel
- Plate, bowl, and silverware for each person
- Drinking cup with measurements marked on the side
- Sauce pan with lid
- Frying pan with non-stick coating
- Teapot or extra saucepan with lid
- Spoon, wooden or slotted
- Spatula
- Wire whisk
- Good slicing knife
- Swiss Army knife with can opener, bottle opener, and cork screw
- Some extra spoons, knives, and forks for cooking tools
- Vegetable peeler
- Cutting board
- Extra plastic bowl with lid

Other items:
- Paper towels
- Aluminum foil
- Salt and pepper
- Other spices
- Cooking oil
- Matches
- Biodegradable dish soap
- Scouring sponge
- Plastic table cloth
- Water filter

For large groups, from five to fifteen people, I like to use a two-burner white gas stove along with a small backpacking gas stove. That way I can prepare dinner on the larger stove and keep hot water for beverages going on the smaller one. For small groups, two small stoves usually work just fine. I use white gas (Coleman fuel) stoves because that's the kind I had when I got my llamas, the fuel is readily available at local supermarkets, and the fuel bottles are lightweight when empty.

Some packers use a two-burner propane stove and a small "four and a half pound" fuel bottle for their trips; the bottle doesn't weigh four and a half pounds - more like eleven when filled. These bottles are a little heavy, but you might want to check out all the options if you're starting from scratch.

Small butane backpacking stoves are sold in outdoor stores and catalogs. They are easy to light, and can work well, but they require many throwaway fuel cartridges, and they don't perform well in cold weather or at high altitudes.

Be sure to take a stove along on your pack trips, rather than relying on fires for cooking all your meals. With the amount of use our backcountry gets these days, using wood for cooking can have a major, long-term negative impact. In addition, some national parks and wilderness areas prohibit campfires. At dry times of year, campfires may be prohibited but stoves acceptable. You have your llama to carry the stove, so take it along. If you have a campfire to sit around, make it small and cozy.

While we're on the subject of low impact camping, be sure to take along plastic garbage bags to pack out your trash. And since the llamas are carrying it, why not take a little time to pack out any extra garbage you may find along the way? It's a good rule to leave any campsite a little better than you found it, and to show as little trace of your visit as possible.

Gravity Flow
Water Filter System

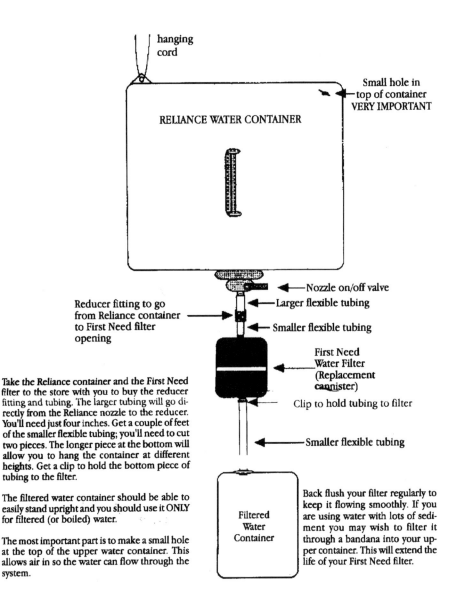

hanging
cord

Small hole in
top of container
VERY IMPORTANT

RELIANCE WATER CONTAINER

Nozzle on/off valve

Reducer fitting to go
from Reliance container
to First Need filter
opening

Larger flexible tubing

Smaller flexible tubing

First Need
Water Filter
(Replacement
cannister)

Take the Reliance container and the First Need filter to the store with you to buy the reducer fitting and tubing. The larger tubing will go directly from the Reliance nozzle to the reducer. You'll need just four inches. Get a couple of feet of the smaller flexible tubing; you'll need to cut two pieces. The longer piece at the bottom will allow you to hang the container at different heights. Get a clip to hold the bottom piece of tubing to the filter.

Clip to hold tubing to filter

Smaller flexible tubing

The filtered water container should be able to easily stand upright and you should use it ONLY for filtered (or boiled) water.

The most important part is to make a small hole at the top of the upper water container. This allows air in so the water can flow through the system.

Filtered
Water
Container

Back flush your filter regularly to keep it flowing smoothly. If you are using water with lots of sediment you may wish to filter it through a bandana into your upper container. This will extend the life of your First Need filter.

In addition to your food list, you may want to make a list of other kitchen gear to take along. Packers are forever making lists. For at least your first few trips, you might want to jot down the essentials. I try to keep everything together in one area at home so it's easy to find. I can tell if I'm forgetting anything by scanning that area before leaving.

Everyone forgets something now and again. I forgot cups and bowls on one commercial trip. Luckily, it was a small, friendly group and we were able to improvise with yogurt cups and other containers. I actually tried to talk a passing boy scout into trading us his cup for a hearty helping of brownies, but he looked a little sad and said he couldn't part with it, as it was part of a set matching his bowl and plate.

Don't forget to bring along dish washing soap, and a scrubbing sponge for after-meal cleanups. You'll want to keep all soap and dirty dish water out of streams and lakes, so bring a container to wash in. Dig a small "gray water" hole near your kitchen area and dispose of your dish water in the hole rather than tossing it (and it's accompanying bits of food and soap) across the landscape.

Since even the most pristine lake or stream may carry the dreaded Giardia protozoa or bacterial contaminants, you should purify your drinking water. You may choose to boil it for three minutes, treat it with iodine tablets, or use a water filter. Several water filters designed for backpackers are sold through outdoor stores. These filters are lightweight and easy to use (The diagram at left shows how to use a First Need® filter to make a gravity flow system for use in camp). Luckily, your llamas won't contract Giardia; they can enjoy their drinking water untreated.

Those who love to cook will enjoy being able to include a few extra utensils in their backcountry kitchen. In addition to a slotted serving spoon, vegetable peeler, and spatula, you may want to pack along a wire whisk, a cup that has measuring gradients, and a cutting board. At least one llama packer has been known to take a battery-operated blender for mixing mai tais. (That same packer has been known to raise llama packing to the heights of hedonism by taking along supplies for a portable sauna.)

You may also want to include a plastic tablecloth in your camp kitchen. This works well as a simple ground cover for laying out kitchen items and keeping them out of the dirt. If you'd like to splurge, and have the extra weight allowance, several outdoor catalogs sell roll-up tables for true dining elegance.

As I've mentioned before, llamas are generally happier if you have two or more animals than if you have just one. When you come to thinking about your kitchen, you may realize that you too would be happier with more llamas. Not only for the pleasures of getting to know the animals, but also for the delicious food they can carry for you! Remember, everything seems to taste better in the back country.

Chapter Twelve
BACKCOUNTRY LLAMA FIRST AID

An ounce of prevention is worth at least a pound of cure when it comes to dealing with sick or injured llamas in the backcountry. If you go into the woods with a well-trained, healthy llama, and if you know something about practical first aid and how to avoid poisonous plants, then chances are that you and your llama will come home safe and sound.

I've discussed the elements of prevention. Begin by conditioning your llama before asking him to carry heavy loads for long distances. Feed him a nutritious diet; maintain a regular vaccination and worming schedule. Make sure his toenails are trimmed, he's sheared adequately for your climate, and that he's used to negotiating a picket line.

Knowing what a healthy llama looks and acts like is a big part of recognizing a sick one. That sounds simple, but llamas are very stoic. Often the clues that one is sick are not obvious. Time spent getting to know each of your llamas, in the field at home and on the trail, is valuable in order to know the norms.

Taking a basic first aid course, if you have never done so or if it has been some time, is a prudent measure. In many instances, you will use general first aid practices to treat backcountry problems of both llamas and humans.

The Llama First Aid Kit
(These items are further discussed in the text.)

- Betadine scrub, swabs or liquid
- Furacin ointment
- Ophthalmic ointment, without steroids
- A non-steroidal anti-inflammatory/analgesic such as injectable Banamine or paste Butazolidin
- Penicillin G Procaine
- Needles (18-gauge) & syringes (20 cc)
- Vet Wrap
- Telfa gauze pads
- 2-inch waterproof adhesive tape
- Duct Tape
- Scissors, tweezers, pliers, knife
- Rectal thermometer
- Superglue
- Piece of sturdy leather or Mt. Sopris Llama Moccasin for padding foot injuries

Optional additions

- Electrolyte replacer—several choices of oral pastes available
- Carmilax
- Activated charcoal
- Two lengths of firm rubber tubing, 1/2 inch outside diameter
- The Extractor
- Hemostat, suture needles, and suture material

The Llama First Aid Kit

The materials listed above are suggested for a llama first aid kit. I strongly recommend going over the list with your vet, adding or omitting items as you see fit. Discuss applications and dosages for any medications you're not familiar with, make some notes, and keep the notes in the kit. If you haven't given injections before, ask a veterinarian to teach you how. Veterinarians who specialize in llamas are now recommending that all injections be given subcutaneously, that is, just below the skin and not into the muscle beneath. Consult your vet for the best site for the injection and the proper technique.

The Betadine scrub comes packaged as swabs or as a liquid. It's used to clean sores or lacerations. The Furacin ointment is antibacterial, for treating minor sores or lacerations. The ophthalmic ointment without steroids is to treat eye injuries.

Banamine and Butazolidin are non-steroidal anti-inflammatories that can be used to reduce inflammation and muscle soreness. You may use injectable Banamine or the paste form of Butazolidin. Do not under any circumstances use injectable Butazolidin.

Penicillin is a useful antibiotic, especially in the case of snakebite. You'll want to keep it in your cooler and have a supply of needles and syringes as well. If you are not concerned with the possibility of snakebite there are other antibiotics in paste form that do not need to stay cool. Check with your vet.

VetWrap is adhesive material that comes in a roll and is used to hold dressings in place. Gauze pads may be used for dressing sores or lacerations. Waterproof adhesive tape will be useful for holding bandages in place and duct tape is especially useful over foot pad injuries.

You probably have scissors, tweezers, pliers and a knife along in your general camping gear. My Swiss Army knife and my indispensable Leatherman tool provide all of these items. Just the same you may choose to keep a small pair of scissors and tweezers in with your first aid kit.

When you purchase a rectal thermometer, get one with a hole in the end, then tie on a sturdy length of string with a clothes pin or alligator clip on the end. When you use the thermometer, attach the clip to the llama's wool to prevent losing the thermometer if it falls out. Leave it in for three minutes. Normal llama temperature is 99 to 102 degrees F.

Superglue can be used to mend a torn nail or superficial pad cut. You can take along a chunk of 1/4 inch leather for padding a lacerated pad or purchase a Mt. Sopris Llamas' "Llama Moccasin" bootie that goes on over the bandaged foot, providing good padding and traction. Their address is in Appendix Seven.

The optional items provide for special packing considerations. An electrolyte replacer is recommended for hot weather packing. There are several commercial paste or granular mixtures available or you may use a mixture of sea salt plus sodium chloride, potassium chloride and magnesium.

Carmilax, a veterinary milk of magnesia product, is used to treat stress-related acidosis (an accumulation of acids brought on by a disturbance in the acid-base balance of the body), and possible plant poisoning. Activated charcoal is also used to treat possible plant poisoning.

If poisonous snakes are a concern where you'll be packing, it's a good idea to carry two lengths of firm rubber tubing and a suction device marketed by Sawyer Products under the name of The Extractor. It may be used on humans or llamas.

Deep lacerations, while uncommon, may occur. If you feel you could make and effort to suture the wound, you may wish to pack along suture needles, suturing material and a hemostat. You may already have both the hemostat and suturing material (monofilament line) in with your fishing gear.

Preparing for potential problems

Before you leave home, spend some time thinking bout the first aid challenges that are most likely to occur and how you would handle them in a remote setting. Then make sure your fist aid kit contains the proper materials for dealing with those situations. Where you hike can make a difference in the type of injuries you are likely to have to treat. If you'll be traveling on volcanic rocks, the llamas' foot pads may be cut. If it's a hot region and your llama is only in fair condition, he'll run the risk of suffering from heat stress. Perhaps rattlesnakes or ticks may be common in the area where you'll be hiking.

You may also want to think about the problems that are not so likely to occur. If your llama is injured to the point that he can carry little or nothing, then you're going to have to improvise a way to carry things yourself. Having a way to convert your panniers into backpacks would be helpful.

A llama that is critically injured is something none of us ever wants to have to deal with or even to think about. However, it is always a possibility. If you do not regularly carry a firearm with you on your pack trips I recommend discussing with your veterinarian other options for putting a critically injured llama out of his misery.

Foot injuries

Foot injuries are one of the most common first aid cases. This is when your pre-trip training can really pay off. If your llama easily allows you to pick up and handle his feet, tending to a cut pad or other foot injury will be much easier. Clean any wound with Betadine or diluted strong iodine, then cover it with Furacin ointment, pad it with gauze, and use your VetWrap to hold the gauze in place. If the cut is on a pad then you'll need to use a chunk of leather and wrap the foot with duct tape in order to keep on hiking. Be sure to clean the wound and replace the dressing daily. A torn toenail may need to be drastically trimmed back, or it may be able to be repaired with Superglue.

Over the years I've had just two llamas come up lame. The first was Coyote who had gone through his early foot-handling lessons with about a C-minus average. But I was glad he'd had them at all when he became lame during a pack trip. On our layover day I noticed that he was barely putting any weight on one of his front feet while he grazed out in the meadow. I caught him and discovered an abscess on the outside of his foot where the hairline meets the edge of the pad. This was actually a relief for me, because I knew there was something I could do to help.

While one of the guests firmly held Coyote, reassuring him that we were really trying to help, I drained the abscess by squeezing the fluid out. Then I washed the area with Betadine and covered it with Furacin. Finally I applied a gauze dressing, wrapped it with VetWrap and covered the works with duct tape. He stood reasonably well for all this fuss and pain.

We loaded his panniers with all the sleeping pads and distributed his original load among the other llamas. He hobbled as he walked, but he never complained.

The next morning Coyote stood calmly as I changed the dressing without assistance. The abscess looked good, and no more fluid was draining so I repeated the washing and bandaging for our hike out. His limp was barely noticeable on that day and by the time we got him to the vet late that afternoon, his limp was completely gone.

On another trip Apollo turned up lame with a very nasty cut on his pad. We'd spent the previous two nights in a popular campsite and I suspect a piece of broken glass or old tin can was to blame. With the help of the two doctors on the trip (one a foot surgeon - her job was to offer him pellets while I cleaned and dressed the wound) I thoroughly irrigated the wound with clean water, then treated it as I had Coyote's foot. This time, though, I used a Mt. Sopris Llama Moccasin, a sturdy little bootie made out of Cordura cloth, with Velcro straps that hold it firmly in place and a durable rubber bottom that provides cushion and traction. It's kind of spendy, but it sure made the difference on that trip.

It took several weeks for Apollo to stop favoring that foot, but the wound healed cleanly and he was able to continue packing later in the summer.

Coyote recovered quickly from his abscessed foot. Here he looks over his shoulder during a pause on the trail.

Saddle sores

If your llama suffers an open sore from a rubbing cinch or a poorly fitting saddle, you may treat the area as you would a cut, trimming away any excess wool, cleaning the wound and applying ointment. You may be able to increase padding to the area. One way is to cut a doughnut out of leather or a piece of ensolite sleeping pad, centering the hole over the wound and securing in place.

Try to identify the cause of the sore. Does the saddle fit your llama poorly? Was there a piece of debris in the wool large enough to rub him raw? As soon as you get home, take any necessary steps to correct problems with ill-fitting equipment and make sure that in the future your cinches and saddle pads are clean and free from debris that may irritate your llama's skin.

Sprains and fractures

Sprains and fractures are most often the result of a llama leaping and then falling off balance. Make sure your animals are trained to walk through creeks, not leap over them. They should also be used to stepping over fallen logs. Take extra care when negotiating any obstacle, especially narrow bridges.

Sprains - injuries to the tendons or ligaments - are most likely to occur in your llama's leg. They will need time to fully heal - about six weeks is common. You'll need to get the injured animal home as soon as possible. You may give him Butazolidin paste or Banamine to lessen the inflammation and make him more comfortable so he'll be able to travel out. His load will have to be considerably lightened.

A fractured bone will need to be splinted, immobilizing the joint above and below the fracture. You may have to improvise splinting materials from what you have on hand. Tent poles and sleeping pads can be used to splint a fracture on a lower leg after you've cleaned, dressed, and padded any external injuries. Keep your dressings loose, as these injuries tend to swell and you don't want to restrict blood flow. Take care that the rigid splinting material is well padded where it may come in contact with the llama. Again, Buazolidin paste or injectable Banamine should be administered for inflammation and pain, and the llama should be led out as soon as possible.

Heat exhaustion

Heat exhaustion can be a problem on extended hot hiking trips, especially if there is high humidity or if the evenings stay warm. An out of shape, overloaded, or extra woolly llama runs a much higher risk of falling victim to heat stress. Heavy mouth breathing, foaming at the mouth, staggering, and general weakness are all alarming signals that your llama is in distress. Check his temperature. If it's elevated, above 103 degrees F, cool him off immediately, using water and/ or snow. If water is limited, apply damp cloths on his less woolly areas. Inside his rear legs is a good spot where there is little fiber and large veins are close to the skin's surface, allowing the cooling action to take effect more quickly. Administer an electrolyte replacer and keep plenty of drinking water available.

This is one situation that is very preventable. Make sure your llama is in condition and shear off any excess wool over three inches in length. In hot weather keep his loads moderate, take an easy pace and watch for signs of overexertion. Keep in mind that a long ride in a small trailer during hot weather may also set llamas up for heat stress. Provide good ventilation and give them time to recover from the ride before asking them to go to work.

Eye injuries

Minor eye injuries may be treated by first carefully removing any foreign matter from the eye. The corner of a clean bandanna can be used in many cases. Again, desensitized llamas will be easier to treat.

In any case, don't use any sharp tool near the eye. If you can't get something out easily, leave it in, as it may wash out on its own. Ophthalmic ointment may be used to treat minor eye injuries. Be sure to use an ointment that does not contain steroids since, if the surface of the eye were scratched, steroids entering the wound could worsen the injury.

Plant poisoning

Llamas like to browse, and to them, the whole wilderness is one great llama delicatessen. Quite often they dive right into the shrubs and flowers, especially if they don't get a big variety in their feed at home. For this reason it's really important that you be aware of the most common poisonous plants that may be found in the area where

Llamas like to browse. To them, the wilderness is a great llama deli. Here, Coyote and Levi take advantage of a short break from hiking. It's up to you to learn the poisonous plants where you hike.

you'll be hiking. Water hemlock and plants in the rhododendron and azalea family are some of the most dangerous. Don't tie your llamas next to or let them browse on any plant you're not sure is safe. Appendix Three lists a number of plants known to be poisonous to livestock.

If your llama shows signs of colic as well as incoordination and extreme salivation, you can suspect that he has eaten something he shouldn't have. You may choose to treat him for plant poisoning by administering Carmilax and, in extreme cases, activated charcoal. Injectable Banamine can also be used to calm an upset stomach that may go along with the poisoning. Most of the time the signs will appear twelve to twenty-four hours after he's eaten the noxious plant. You'll need to stay put until he's recovered and able to travel again.

Snake bite

If you'll be traveling into areas where poisonous snakes are common, you'll want to take extra precautions in the form of vaccinations and additional first aid items. Llamas do not have a natural fear of snakes and, since they are very curious, they may stick their nose right into trouble. A venomous snake bite on a llama's face can be especially dangerous if it swells and blocks the nasal airway. For this reason you should have a couple of eight to twelve inch long sections of stiff rubber tubing, about 1/2 inch in outside diameter, to insert in your llama's nostrils. Some types of water filter tubing may work well for this purpose.

A secondary complication to snake bite can come in the form of a clostridial infection at the wound site. Vaccinating your llamas for malignant edema will help lower the risk of this problem. Most seven and eight way vaccines contain this element. Check with your vet if you're unsure. You'll also want to carry a 100 cc bottle of aqueous solution Penicillin G Procaine and administer 20cc subcutaneously, two times a day. Keep the animal quiet to avoid spreading toxins through his system and walk him out as soon as possible, recognizing that it may take a day or two for him to stabilize to the point where he can travel safely.

Ticks

Ticks are often a problem early in the summer, especially in brushy country. If an infected female tick carrying the disease attaches and becomes engorged, llamas can contract tick paralysis. The signs to look for are a seemingly sudden onset of incoordination, anxiety and flaccid paralysis. If left untreated, this disease can be fatal. The up side is that llamas quickly recover when the offending tick is removed. It will be easier to find an embedded tick on a short-wooled llama, so shearing is once again recommended. Make sure the recovering llama has access to plenty of fluids and you should seek additional veterinary treatment as soon as you get home.

As a preventative measure you can carry a spray bottle of Ectrin solution, spraying the llamas' legs, chest, belly and haunches at least once a day. To date, Lyme disease, spread by a different type of tick and quite common in some parts of the country, has not been diagnosed in llamas.

Other problems

Porcupines can pose a danger for our overly curious llamas. If you find quills in your llama you'll be glad you brought along a pair of pliers (the Leatherman tool is an especially handy llama packing item) with which to remove them. Pliers can also be used to remove cactus thorns. In both instances you should clean the wound site with Betadine and apply Furacin ointment.

I've never heard of a llama getting poison oak or poison ivy, but sensitive people could get a case from touching the llama's wool after the animal had been walking through the plants. Most of my

Hiking down the lush trail along Saddle Creek in Hells Canyon, we stay alert for poison ivy and rattlesnakes.

packing is into an area with no poison oak or ivy so I haven't had this experience. But I have friends who insisted that I mention a product for people: Tecnu is available over the counter in pharmacies. My friends take it with them into the backcountry for washing themselves, with or without water, to remove the oils. It can also be used to relieve the itching if a rash should develop.

If your llama becomes ill or injured to the extent that he is unable to walk out for treatment, then you are going to have to make some very hard decisions. Perhaps you will be able to leave one member of your party with the animal while you go out to seek medical help and supplies. If you are traveling alone, you may have to leave him unattended while you go out for help. Be sure he has access to water, either from a bucket or a natural source, while you're gone.

Chances are that you will not have to administer much first aid, especially if your llamas are in good condition and well trained to start with. Remember that ounce of prevention.

Chapter Thirteen
STARTING A COMMERCIAL PACK BUSINESS

After you've been ambling through the wilderness a while with your wooly companions, you may think that you'd like to try turning your love of llamas and the outdoors into a commercial business. You're getting interested in the idea of leading llama pack trips, sharing your enthusiasm with other folks, and getting paid for it to boot. There are a number of things you'll want to consider before starting a career as a *llamero*.

As in beginning any business, you should sit down and decide what your goals are going to be. Do you want to make llama packing your main job? What kind of trips do you want to offer? Maybe you want to confine your business to just packing people's gear in and out, rather than offering a complete backcountry catering service. Perhaps you'd like to offer one-day trips to spread the "good news" you've experienced from your enjoyment of llamas. Your first task will be to outline what you think you want to do. Consider what you want to get out of it, both financially and personally.

Guiding backcountry trips is more than hiking with your llamas through great mountain scenery for pay. All outfitters worth their salt have to be part business person, part fearless leader, part chief cook and bottle washer, part baby sitter, part psychologist, and part llama skinner - perhaps in that order. Outfitting the public is a service requiring business sense, leadership skills, organization, and very hard work. You'd better be a person with a high energy level. And if you're not an outstanding cook, hiring someone who is could add significantly to the success of your venture from word-of-mouth referrals.

Anyone leading outdoor trips has to be knowledgeable about wilderness camping skills, first aid, and animal handling. It takes organization and attention to detail to cope with schedules, reservations, and business concerns as well as the myriad details of the trips themselves.

A guide needs sensitivity and patience to deal with the many different demands of the guests and to answer the same questions over and over with enthusiasm. Guests will often need to be shown how to conduct themselves in the backcountry, how to handle the llamas, and perhaps even how to have a good time - especially when weather and trail conditions are less than perfect. Many people who go on commercial llama pack trips have little or no previous experience in the backcountry.

You will need to be flexible, too. Clients will come with many different interests and levels of skill. Sometimes routes or schedules may need to be altered in the middle of a trip to handle one person's needs. A guest or a llama may be injured and necessitate a decision to layover an extra day. It's not possible to plan for every situation, but with ingenuity and improvisation, problems can be solved and a trip made even more memorable.

Good backcountry skills are essential. When leading large groups into the wilderness, you will be responsible for keeping environmental impact to a minimum. Guides should educate their clients in proper disposal of trash and human waste, as well as in how to leave as clean a camp as possible.

A solid pack string of well-trained llamas is a vital part of a commercial packing business. The llamas must be able to be handled by novices - and they must willingly follow the hikers - often out of sight and reach of the outfitter. Fortunately, llamas' natural abilities will make this one of the easier requirements to fulfill.

How you'll make money

When planning your new business, consider what types of trips to offer. Picnic day hikes, fully-outfitted trips, drop camp or spot packing services, and renting llamas out have been successful for other packers. They all have their positive aspects and their limitations.

Guests on a commercial pack trip are people with a variety of interests and skills. Some have never been in the backcountry before.

Picnic hikes are a quick, enjoyable way to share your enthusiasm for llamas with a wide variety of other people. The planning, preparation, and actual outings are less work than for overnight trips. Day hikes don't bring in a large income, though, and they still require expensive liability insurance when they take place on public lands. Some llama owners in different parts of the country have offered day hikes on their own land, as an adjunct to their ranch operation.

Fully-outfitted trips bring in the largest gross income. They also require the largest financial investment in promotion, animals, and equipment. There is a lot of work, both physical and mental, in scheduling, packing, and providing for the needs of the clients. There is also a lot of demand for this type of trip.

Drop camps are simple to operate, but the demand for them is not as high as for other types of trips. The income is less, but expensive insurance is still necessary. Renting llamas out can be simple too, but not many packers are ready to send their wooly friends out into the backcountry with strangers. Those who do usually require that the people renting the llamas attend one or more training sessions first. Sometimes, rented llamas are ones available for sale, and the rental process is a way for the hikers to see if they want to own llamas.

How you'll spend money

When you decide what types of services to offer, you will have to consider how many llamas and how much equipment you will need to operate your trips. The costs of acquiring and feeding animals, and the costs of their packs and other gear, should be figured into your budget.

If you need eight llamas to run scheduled trips all summer, will you have room to keep them all at home, or will you have to rent pasture or buy more land?

Will you be providing tents and group camping gear? That's another expense for the budget.

Transportation costs will be affected by the distances you must cover to reach the area where you'll be packing. If you will be traveling quite a ways to reach the trailhead, take that into account when deciding what to charge for your services. If you need to haul more than a couple of llamas, then you'll have to have a truck or trailer capable of accommodating all your critters, the gear, and maybe even the people.

Depending on the trips you offer and your personal situation, it may be necessary to hire employees to assist with your business. For safety reasons, it is best to have at least two guides for every party. Many packers have friends who enjoy helping out in exchange for getting to go along, while some packers hire one or more paid employees for the whole season.

Any business has a variety of office expenses. You'll need to plan for phone, postage, brochure, and other promotional costs. And depending on your situation, there may be legal fees to draw up corporation or partnership documents.

It's hard to predict how soon you might break even, so consider a range of possibilities in planning how much capital you'll need to begin with.

Permits, licenses, and insurance

Where you pack is a big decision. You'll have to investigate the necessity and the availability of outfitting permits in any area you consider. Some Forest Service and Park Service districts place a limit on the number of commercial outfitters they allow. And even if you can get a permit, there may already be another llama packer in the area. If so, is there enough demand for the service to keep two packers busy?

Anyone making money on public lands must have a special use permit. Obtaining a permit is no small feat; in some areas, it may be virtually impossible. The regulating agencies are usually the National Forest Service, the Bureau of Land Management, and the National Park Service. If you overcome the paperwork hurdle and are able to get a permit, there is a fee for it. Forest Service and B.L.M. permit fees are based on the amount of money the outfitter collects from his clients. In a National Park, it is usually a set fee per season. Grazing fees and your use of specially designated campsites can add to the amount of money the agency will charge. In addition, any of the agencies will require that the outfitter have liability insurance naming the government as coinsured.

Be sure to thoroughly investigate the requirements for permits and insurance before you commit any significant amount of capital to your proposed endeavor. Contact the appropriate Forest Service district or Park Service office for detailed information on regulations and fees. Be sure to find out how long the process will take, as well. For insurance, the agencies may have some information, or check with other llama packers.

In addition to the federal agencies, you may have to deal with your state. Many states require licenses for commercial outfitters. You'll need to find out if a license is necessary to operate in your state, and if so, what requirements must be met in order to obtain one.

In case you're contemplating just taking to the woods without all this bureaucratic hassle, a word of warning. The backcountry may seem remote, but the people who use the backcountry in a region form a network of friends and acquaintances. News travels fast, and your presence will not be a secret.

Professional pack llamas must be able to be led by novices and must willingly follow their hikers.

Marketing

Numerous books have been written on successful business marketing techniques. A few of the basics are covered here, to try to point you in the right direction for this specific business.

When you're thinking about what types of trips to offer, you should also be considering who will be your clients. Where will they come from, what will their interests be, and how can you reach them?

I told you there was more to this than hiking in the woods.

Brochures and advertising in magazines are two common, and relatively expensive, promotional techniques. Some less expensive ways for people to learn about your business include word of mouth, articles in newspapers and magazines, and human interest spots on television and radio.

A brochure should include the essential information about your services: what you offer, where, when, and how much it costs. It's a job for a professional to create a pleasing and interesting brochure. Unless you have skills in producing promotional literature, you will want to hire some assistance in designing the brochure. Printing costs and quality vary quite a bit from printer to printer, so be sure to get a few estimates and samples of their work before choosing a firm to print your brochure. Like everyone else, printers sometimes run late, so don't make your schedule so tight that a few extra days will give you high blood pressure.

Advertising is an expensive way to promote your business, but a carefully designed ad campaign can generate a lot of clients and produce a good mailing list. Target your advertising to the audience that will be most likely to be interested in what you offer - active people who enjoy the outdoors. Repetition of your ads is important, too. One ad once a year in a magazine is a waste of money. You'll need to

An attractive brochure will help you sell your pack trips.

budget for several well-timed ads, concurrent in several magazines, so people will see them more than once and think of you when they think about a hiking vacation.

Web sites are an excellent way to get the word out. A huge number of people are using the web to find more information on travel opportunities. Make sure your site is attractive, not too complex, and well-indexed. If you don't spend money or time on indexing your site, no one will find you and your web expenses are wasted.

Be timely. Don't advertise in October for trips the following July, but don't wait until May, either. Many people work for companies that require them to select their summer leave time in January.

Save the names and addresses of everyone who responds to an ad, and build a mailing list for the future, on a computer if available. Many people will inquire one year and go on a trip the next. Then, if they have a good time, they'll tell their friends about it, and in a few years you may not need to advertise at all. Word of mouth is very effective.

One article applauding your operation in a newspaper or magazine can do as much good as several advertisements. If you offer something unique, such as travel to an interesting area or a special kind of trip, you may be able to get some free publicity. By now, simply packing with llamas is not going to be unique enough for most magazines, but should warrant an article in your local newspaper.

You may want to contact hiking or other outdoor groups about putting together a trip for their members. A nice slide show or a quality video with personal narration can be a good way to sell your trips to groups.

If you're providing a quality service and are creative in your marketing approach, you'll have the best chance for success.

Participation in local parades can help get the word out about your business.

A few other ideas

Talk to a lawyer when you are setting up your business, and work with him or your liability insurance company to draw up a liability release. This is a form that your clients sign, absolving you of responsibility in the event of a mishap. Many people will say that a release is not worth the paper it's printed on, however a well-worded release that truly defines the activities and the risks involved, including death, can provide a defense, will make the clients think about what they are embarking on, and it may prevent a whimsical legal action. No release will protect you for your own personal negligence, though, so make pre-trip and on-site orientation instructions thorough; have safety in mind when carrying out your campsite selection and procedures; and be sure your llamas are well-mannered and up to the tasks at hand.

If you plan a series of scheduled trips, start out with easier routes so your llamas can get into shape at the beginning of the season.

Participate in fairs and local festivals, especially when you're getting started, to get the word out about your trips.

Always keep a supply of brochures in your car, and take some with you on your trips. You just might meet a weary hiker who is ready to exchange a heavy backpack for a llama and a light day pack on another outing!

Get to know other commercial llama packers. If there are llama packers in the region you will be using, be sure to contact them. There's nothing like experience, and most are more than willing to share what they've learned.

If you'll be packing into an area that is used by commercial horse packers, it's a good idea to get to know them. Offer to lend them a llama to put next to their horses and mules for a few days. This will allow the other animals to become more accustomed to the sight and smell of a llama. By doing this, you can lower the possibility of a negative encounter in the backcountry while building some goodwill with the other outfitters.

Be sure you don't put your llama right in with the horses and mules. Llamas don't have any real defense against the sharp hooves and teeth of the larger animals; a wad of cud wouldn't do much to deter an argumentative mule. It works best to leave the llama in a pen adjacent to the field or corral where the horses are kept. A few days is long enough.

You should definitely expect a lot of good-natured kidding from the horse packer contingent. Try not to mention how llama dung doesn't smell. Let the horse packers notice how little a llama eats,

Murphy and Billy are obstacles for a mule show trail class. The first year llamas participated, only a few mules walked between the tethered llamas. The next year, only a few mules didn't.

and watch their faces as you hop the llama up into the truck to take him home. You don't need to broadcast the virtues of owning llamas; the animals themselves will get the point across with much more subtlety.

Cupcake has been my goodwill ambassador on several occasions. At one outfitter's ranch, I left him picketed next to the horses' feeding area for a couple of days. The horses didn't really want to get close to him at first, but finally their hunger drove them to the feeder. They adjusted to him very quickly. Another time we left him in an adjacent corral next to a mule packer's string, and that worked well too. He even spent several months one winter at a horse outfitter's ranch, and ended up charming the packer to the point that now the man has his own young llama he's hoping to work into his pack string for summer trips!

I'm very glad I started my llama packing business, and I'm making a significant part of my living from it - but I have friends who tried it for a few seasons, lost a little money or made something under minimum wage, and quit. Give the idea plenty of thought and do your research thoroughly before joining the ranks of the commercial packers.

Appendix One:
RUBBER BAND CONNECTOR
PACK BAG PATTERN AND DIRECTIONS

Rubber Band Connector

Safety dictates that some sort of weak link or quick release system be used when connecting two or more llamas in a string.

An effective, inexpensive way to accomplish this is to use a No. 107 heavy duty rubber band (7 x 1/16 x 5/8 in.) as a connecting weak link. It will stretch to accommodate llamas that are tardy to follow up, or it will break if a really strong force is applied to it. The rubber bands are lightweight, can often be retied to use through more than one break, and packers can easily keep a few extra in their pocket or day pack for quick replacement.

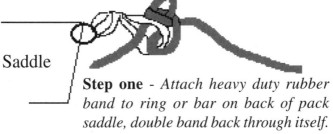

Saddle

Step one - *Attach heavy duty rubber band to ring or bar on back of pack saddle, double band back through itself.*

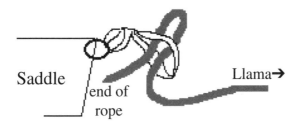

Saddle

end of rope

Llama→

Step two - *Insert loop of lead rope up through loop in rubber band.*

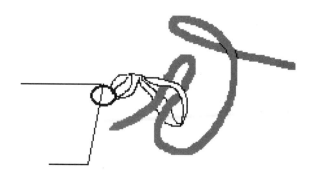

Steps three and four - *Make a twist in the lead rope between the part inserted through the rubber band and the llama, and place it down over the loop, pulling tight on the slack.*

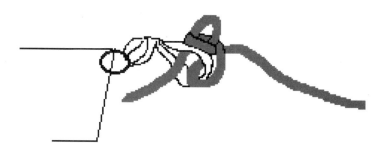

To release, simply unsnug the locking loop.

Pack Bag Pattern and Directions

These directions will make one pair of pack bags to sling on a frame style pack saddle. Finished dimensions are approximately 22" wide, 10" deep and 17" tall. You may want to make adjustments to fit your own camping gear such as a cooler or cook box. Three yards of corduroy will allow for slightly larger bags.

Materials List

3 yds.	11 oz. coated corduroy - 60" wide
4 ft.	2 in. wide nylon webbing - seat belt webbing or similar
16 yds.	1 in. wide nylon webbing
4 yds.	1/8 inch nylon cord for drawstring closure
4 ft.	1 in. wooden dowel
8	1 in. wide Fastex side release buckles
4	1 in. ladderlock buckles
2	mini or maxi toggles
24	grommets

Heavy Duty Sewing Machine Needles
Strong Nylon or Poly Thread
Marking Chalk

Material Sources

The Green Pepper
941 Olive St.
Eugene, OR 97401

Moore Manufacturing Co.
Box 321
Skykomish, WA 98288

Please note: Be sure to sear all ends of nylon webbing and cord over flame to prevent fraying. A candle works well for this purpose.

Directions

1. Cut the following out of 1" webbing:
   - 4 Pieces 76" long for Compression Straps
     Includes extra allowance to attach tents or pads under strap
   - 4 Pieces 32" long for Sling Straps
     Includes extra allowance for tying on top loads with strap ends
   - 4 Pieces 11" long for Bag Lower Corner Straps
   - 4 Pieces 6" long for Flap Corner Straps

2. For Hanging and Weighing straps, cut one piece of 1" webbing 19" long; then cut that piece in half lengthwise. For bag back - ing, cut 2 pieces 22" long of 2" wide nylon webbing. Make sure to sear all edges with heat.

3. Sew Fastex buckles to compression and sling straps by threading one and a half inches of the strap through the male end of the buckle, and stitching an "x" inside a rectangle pattern through the double thickness of webbing.

4. Attach a ladderlock buckle to each flap corner strap: thread the strap through the male end of the buckle, double the strap, place the buckle in the fold, and paste in place.

5. Cut the four foot length of dowel into two pieces 22" long.

6. Cut two lengths of 1/8" cord two yards long for the draw string closure.

7. Cut out bag: on right side of fabric, mark in chalk the lines indicating the inside corner, lower corner allowances (bold lines) and compression strap keeper placement.

8. Sew bag corner straps in place.

9. Sew strap keepers in place leaving just over one inch spacing for compression strap to pass through easily.

10. With right sides together, join B1 to A and sew along diagonal (bold line). Sew again over first stitching. Repeat, joining B2 to A and sew along diagonal (bold line). Repeat stitching. Take care not to catch corner strap in stitching. Trim away excess fabric to 1/4 inch. Repeat on other side. This is the trickiest part of making the bag. This step forms the rectangular bottom of the bag. If you're confused, look at the picture of the finished bag.

11. Sew side seams. Repeat stitching 1/8 inch outside original seam or fold over and top stitch seam flat. Reinforce the point where all three seams meet with a bar tack.

12. Turn top edge under 3/4 inch and stitch.

216

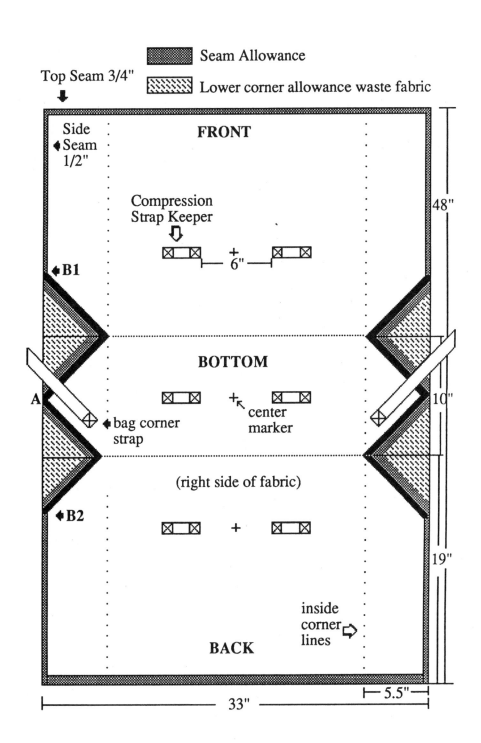

Seam Allowance

Lower corner allowance waste fabric

Top Seam 3/4"

Side
Seam
1/2"

FRONT

Compression
Strap Keeper

6"

B1

BOTTOM

A

bag corner
strap

center
marker

(right side of fabric)

B2

inside
corner
lines

BACK

48"

10"

19"

5.5"

33"

217

DOWEL FLAP

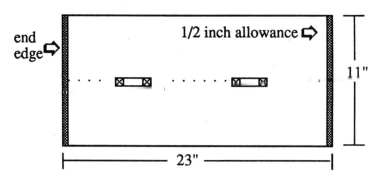

end edge ⇨

1/2 inch allowance ⇨

11"

23"

13. Cut out dowel flap 11" x 23" and stitch strap keepers in place. Turn edges under 1/2 inch and stitch. With wrong sides together, fold entire flap in half and stitch two inches from folded edge.

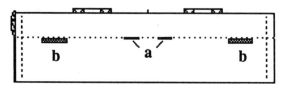

b   a   b

14. Make two 1" buttonholes below stitching line at **"a."**
Make two 1 1/2" buttonholes below stitching line at **"b."**

15. Attach weighing and hanging strap to dowel flap through small buttonholes and secure with cross stiching.

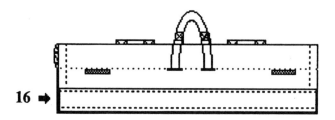

16 ➡

16. Stitch 22" length of two inch wide nylon webbing to dowel flap flush with raw edge.

TOP FLAP

17.   Cut out top flap 23" x 19". Turn under 1/4" on two long and one short side. Stitch. Place compression strap keepers six inches from bottom stitched edge and sew in place.

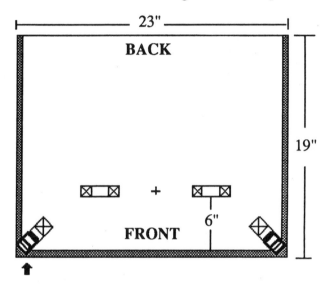

18.   Attach straps with ladderlock buckles to corners of top flap.

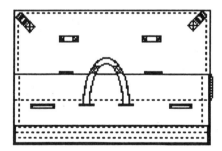

Secure dowel to top flap with basting stitches so that may be attached to the pack bag as one unit.

BAG ASSEMBLY

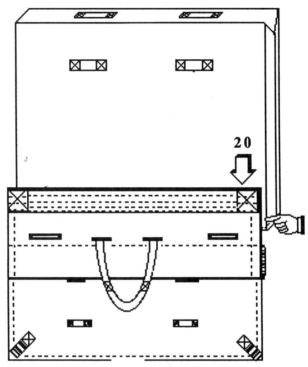

19. Position top and dowel flaps on back of pack bag.

     The closest edge of nylon webbing should be two inches from top edge of bag to allow for drawstring closure.

20. Make four rows of stitching around and through the middle of the nylon webbing. Make large X's on each end of the webbing for reinforcement.

21. Insert dowel into dowel flap and secure with three small nails.

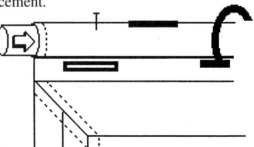

FINISHING TOUCHES

22.   Attach twelve grommets to top edge of bag. Insert draw string in grommet **A** and thread through other holes, finishing at grommet **B**.

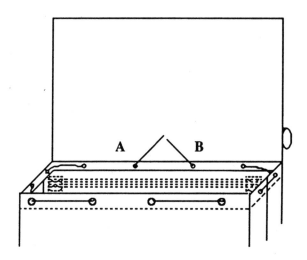

23.   Attach toggle to drawstring.

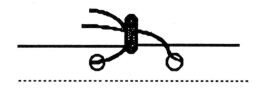

24.   Attach sling straps to bag through large buttonholes below dowel.

25.   Attach compression straps to bag with buckles below top flap keepers in front of bag.

ASSEMBLED BAG

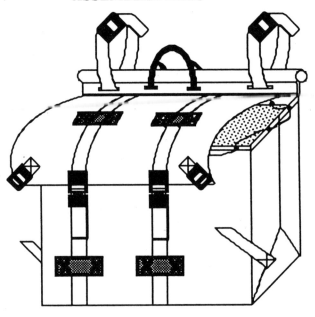

Appendix Two:
RECIPES FOR THE CAMP KITCHEN

Breakfasts

Homemade Granola

While there are lots of granolas on the market, I've never found one that tastes as good as this recipe. Make it up at home and keep it in the freezer until you're ready to go. I enjoy it most with vanilla yogurt and blueberries, raisins, or dates mixed in. It's packed with nutrition and energy. One cup is a hefty serving.

INGREDIENTS:
3 cups oats
2 cups puffed cereal (wheat, rice or millet)
1 cup each of the following:
whole wheat flour
nonfat dry milk
shredded or flaked coconut
unsalted sunflower seeds
wheat germ
chopped walnuts
chopped almonds
chopped cashews
Sesame seeds

AT HOME: Mix the above ingredients together in a large bowl. In a small bowl combine:

1 cup salad oil
1 cup honey
2 teaspoons cinnamon

Pour this mixture over the oats, seeds and nuts, stirring until evenly moistened. Spread the mixture on two large 10 x 15 inch baking pans. Bake in a 250° oven, stirring every fifteen minutes, until it is a deep golden color—about 1 to 1 1/4 hours.

Let it cool completely before placing it in an airtight container. Freeze for longer storage. Makes just under four quarts.

Breakfast Quiche

I'd like to thank Toni Landis for this recipe. It's great for a quick breakfast when you want to get on the trail early. The leftovers are also tasty as lunch snacks or hors d'oeuvres. By using a tortilla, you can freeze the quiche without having the crust go soggy. Let it thaw overnight, heat it up, and serve with fresh fruit and muffins brought from home. Don't be afraid to experiment with ingredients. Try replacing the chilies with cooked sausage or sautéed mushrooms, onions and peppers. Serves up to six.

INGREDIENTS:
3 eggs
1 cup sour cream
1 cup each shredded cheddar and Monterey jack cheese
1 small can green chilies
salt and pepper to taste
1 large tortilla

AT HOME: Preheat oven to 350°. Thoroughly blend the eggs, sour cream, chilies, salt and pepper. Fold in the cheeses. Place the tortilla in a lightly oiled aluminum pie pan, and then add egg mixture. Bake for 40 minutes or until center is firm. Cool completely, cover with two pieces of foil, label and freeze.

IN CAMP: Thaw quiche. Heat slowly on a griddle or over a pan of simmering water. Serve warm.

Hot Cereal Supreme

This recipe will convert most non-oatmeal eaters. It's especially welcome on a cold morning.

INGREDIENTS:
rolled oats or seven grain cereal, 1/3 cup (dry) per serving
dried fruit (bring apples & raisins and add any leftovers from lunches)
nuts (raid your trail mix bag: walnuts, pecans and sunflower seeds are good)
brown sugar or honey, to taste
1 tablespoon dried milk per serving
1 tablespoon butter per serving
cinnamon, to taste
yogurt or cream

AT HOME: Package cereal with dried fruit; label.

IN CAMP: Bring a pan of lightly salted water to boil. Use slightly more water than twice the amount of dry cereal. Stir cereal into boiling water and reduce heat. Begin stirring in additional ingredients as the cereal cooks. Start with the nuts, then the fruit, then add the sweetener, dry milk, and butter. Finish with a dash of cinnamon. After five minutes, remove from heat and cover briefly. Top with any leftover fresh fruit, yogurt, or half and half.

Low Fat Whole Wheat Date Scones

These durable breakfast treats travel well. After I make them at home, I wrap them in foil and then in a plastic bag for travel. In camp I warm them on the back of the stove while cooking breakfast.

225

INGREDIENTS:
1 1/2 cups unbleached flour
1/2 cup whole wheat flour
1/4 cup wheat bran
1/4 cup packed brown sugar
1 1/2 tsp. each baking powder and baking soda
2 tsp. cinnamon
1/2 tsp. salt
2/3 cup chopped dates
3 T. chilled butter cut in small pieces
2/3 cup vanilla yogurt
2 egg whites, lightly beaten

AT HOME: In a large bowl combine first 8 ingredients, then cut in butter. Add dates & toss well. Add yogurt and egg whites, stirring just to moisten. Turn dough onto lightly floured board, knead lightly 3 or 4 times. Pat into 8 inch circle on coated baking sheet. Cut into 10 wedges, not clear through. Bake 350° for 25 minutes or until the loaf sounds hollow.

Orange Pancakes

For a special breakfast pack along a fresh orange and then add the grated peel along with the juice to your favorite instant pancake mix.

Dinners

Chicken, Pepper and Walnut Stir Fry

This dish is without a doubt the most popular meal on my commercial pack trips. I serve it with rice, fresh melon slices and fortune cookies for dessert. I use white Basmati rice because it cooks in just

15 minutes and has a nutty flavor. Brown rice works just fine, but takes three times as long to cook.

INGREDIENTS:
1/3 cup dry white or brown rice per serving 1 or 2 chicken bouillon cubes
1/2 chicken breast per serving
1/2 tablespoon soy sauce per serving
1/2 teaspoon corn starch per serving
1/4 teaspoon fresh ginger per serving
1/4 c walnuts per serving
1/2 green pepper per serving
cooking oil (in camp)

AT HOME: Package rice and bouillon cubes together and label. Mark on bag the amount of water needed for the rice. (This varies depending on the kind of rice you're using; check the package if you aren't sure.) De-bone and slice chicken into thin strips. Mix together soy sauce and corn starch. Pour over chicken and stir together. Chop ginger and wrap in plastic. Place nuts in plastic bag. Place chicken in plastic container, add walnuts and ginger in their wrappings. Label and freeze.

Blend the following cooking sauce ingredients thoroughly, place in small container, label and refrigerate until you go. (It will keep unrefrigerated for 4-5 days). Per serving combine:

1/4 teaspoon cornstarch
dash Tabasco
1/2 teaspoon sugar
1/2 teaspoon dry sherry or water
1/2 tablespoon soy sauce.

Right before you're ready to go, seed and chop the pepper in one inch squares. Package in a Ziploc, with as much air removed as possible, and keep cool. If it's not a staple in your cook kit, be sure to add some cooking oil to prepare this dish. I like to add a little sesame oil to spice it up.

IN CAMP: Make sure your chicken is thawed before dinner time. The stir fry takes about fifteen to twenty minutes to prepare, so put your rice on, then heat a small amount of oil in a wide fry pan. Add the walnuts to the hot oil, and stir fry for two or three minutes. Remove them and then add the peppers and ginger; fry them for two or three minutes more, until bright green. Remove and add the chicken, stirring until opaque. Return the other ingredients to the pan and add the cooking sauce. Stir this a minute or two until the sauce thickens. Serve hot over a bed of rice.

Mexican Spiced Beef

I serve this shredded beef mixture on a tortilla with a selection of condiments including salsa, guacamole, grated cheese and fresh cilantro. This recipe serves ten. You can use it to make enough to freeze for a couple trips.

INGREDIENTS:
About 4 1/2 pounds bone-in beef chuck
3 T. Chili powder
1 T. oregano leaves
1 - 8 oz. can stewed tomatoes
1 -7 oz. can diced green chilies
2 cloves minced garlic
salt & cayenne to taste

Place the roast on a sheet of foil and mix the chilies, chili powder, oregano and garlic; spread on top of roast. Pull foil up around roast and seal. Place in a roasting pan and bake in a 300° oven for 4 to 41/2 hours or until meat is so tender it falls apart.

Unwrap meat; discard fat and bones. Transfer meat and drippings to a large pan and stir in the tomatoes. Heat until hot throughout; stir in salt and cayenne to taste.

Freeze in Ziploc bag and then pack in cooler with condiments for first or second night's dinner. Warm in pan over low flame, adding a little water if necessary. Tortillas can be wrapped in foil at home, packed with dry goods, then warmed over the back of the stove while heating beef mixture.

Lemon Basil Chicken

This is a simple yet gourmet dinner dish that is easy to fix in camp with a little preparation at home. I have used the left over lemon basil butter sauce to fry up fresh trout for the following morning's breakfast. Delicious. This recipe makes four servings.

INGREDIENTS:
4 T. butter or margarine
2 whole chicken breasts, about 2 lbs. total
1 chicken bouillon cube
2 T. grated lemon peel
3 T. chopped fresh bail leaves or 1 T. dry basil
2 T. lemon juice

AT HOME: Split chicken breasts and remove skin and bone or buy frozen skinless, boned breasts. Wrap in plastic and place in Ziploc bag. Freeze solid. Grate lemon peel, juice lemon and put both in small plastic container with chopped basil. Pack in cooler along with butter. Pack bouillon cube with dry goods.

IN CAMP: Thaw chicken breasts. Fry in one tablespoon of butter over medium high heat. Cook until lightly browned on both sides. Meanwhile add bouillon cube to one cup boiling water. Add this along with lemon basil mixture to chicken. Reduce heat, cover, and simmer just until meat in thickest portion of chicken breast is no longer pink, about ten minutes. Remove chicken and keep warm. Bring cooking liquid to boil and cook for about a minute, reducing the mixture to about two thirds. Add remaining 3 tablespoons butter and stir until melted. Serve sauce over chicken.

Zesty Carrot Slaw

Fresh salads in the wilderness are a real treat. Here's an easy one that goes with a variety of main course offerings. This recipe makes 4-5 servings.

INGREDIENTS:
1 1/2 lbs. carrots
1 T. grated lime peel
1/3 c. fresh lime juice
2 T. honey or brown sugar
2 T. distilled vinegar
1 T. Dijon mustard
1/4 T. crushed red chilis
salt to taste

AT HOME: Peel and grate carrots coarsely. Pack in Ziploc bag and keep cool. Mix together remaining ingredients and place in plastic container. Keep cool (dressing mixture can be frozen in advance.)

IN CAMP: Mix carrots and dressing. Salt to taste and serve.

For the sweet tooth

Peach Schnapps Cake

This dense pound cake type dessert packs really well and is a definite treat after a day of hiking. I make it up at home in bread loaf pans, and freeze it. It keeps well in a pack for 5-6 days. Take along some powdered sugar to sprinkle on top, if you like.

INGREDIENTS:
1 package yellow cake mix
1 package vanilla instant pudding mix
3/4 cup oil
1 cup Peach Schnapps
1 cup broken nut meats (pecans are good)

AT HOME: Preheat oven to 325°. Grease and flour two loaf pans. Mix cake mix, pudding mix, eggs, Schnapps and oil on high speed for four minutes. Fold in the nuts and pour into loaf pans. Bake for 50-60 minutes or until a toothpick comes out clean. Cool in pans for 10 minutes. Then remove and place on wire racks. Cool completely, wrap in foil or plastic, label and freeze.

Variations: I've enjoyed playing with the recipe a little. Devils food cake mix, Peppermint schnapps and almonds were great together. The combination of white cake mix, cherry kirsch and almonds was also a hit. Be bold.

Cream Cheese Brownies

These little treats are favorite lunch bag additions. Use a good brownie mix or your favorite "from scratch" recipe, and just add the cream cheese topping. Remember, it takes a little longer to bake with the topping.

> INGREDIENTS:
> *1 box brownie mix (2 if using "Jiffy" brand)*
> *2 T. softened butter*
> *3 oz. softened cream cheese*
> *1/4 cup sugar*
> *1 egg*
> *1 T. flour*
> *1/2 tsp. vanilla*

AT HOME: Prepare brownies as directed on box or with your favorite recipe that fills an 8x8 inch pan. I take two boxes of Jiffy Brownie Mix, substitute coffee extract for the water, and then follow the rest of the directions on the box. Pour batter into prepared pan.

For the topping, thoroughly blend butter with cream cheese. Gradually add sugar, beating well. Add egg, flour and vanilla, blend well. Pour topping over brownie mix and bake as directed adding an extra 10-15 minutes. Variation: If you like mint and chocolate, add 1/8 teaspoon peppermint extract to the cream cheese mixture.

Appendix Three:
A SELECTED LIST OF POISONOUS PLANTS

Listed below is a selection of plants that are commonly found across the country. If eaten, these may affect your llamas. The browsing habits of llamas - a bite here, a bite there usually keep them from consuming enough of a toxic plant to make them ill. But if they are picketed next to a patch of laurel shrubs, they may eat enough leaves to make them quite sick. Appendix Four lists some poisonous plant guidebooks that can help you identify any of the plants that you are unfamiliar with; also check your public library. State extension agents will also have information on poisonous plants in your area.

The following list was compiled by Dr. Murray E. Fowler and is here reprinted, with permission, from the January/February 1985 issue of 3-L Llama, now Llamas Magazine.

POISONOUS PLANTS THAT MAY AFFECT LLAMAS			
PLANT COMMON NAME	PLANT SCIENTIFIC NAME	SIGNS OF POISONING	HABITAT
Arrowgrass	Triglochin maritima	Muscle twitching, convulsions, bright red blood, difficult breathing	Meadows at low to moderate elevations
False hellebore, corn lily	Veratrum ornicum	Vomiting, salivation, convulsions, fast & irregular heartbeat	High mountain meadows
Death camas, sandcorn	Zigadenus spp	Foaming at mouth, convulsions, ataxia, vomiting, fast and weak pulse	Hillsides, fields, meadows, in spring of year

PLANT COMMON NAME	PLANT SCIENTIFIC NAME	SIGNS OF POISONING	HABITAT
Nightshade	Solanum spp	Vomiting, weakness, groaning	Ubiquitous
Jimsonweed, thornapple	Datura meteloides	Dry mouth membranes, dilated pupil, mania	Waste places
Western sneezeweed	Helenium hoopesii	Vomiting, depression, frothing at mouth, coughing, weak irregular pulse	High mountain meadows
Labrador tea	Ledum glandulosum	Vomiting, colic, weakness, loss of appetite, muscle twitches	Around lakes, meadows, streams
Black laurel, Mountain laurel	Leucothoe davisiae	Same as above	Same as above
Western azalea	Rhododendron occidentale	Same as above	Same as above
Rhododendron	Rhododendron spp	Same as above	Same as above
Oleander	Nerium oleander	Diarrhea, colic, cardiac irregularities, blue membranes of mouth	Ornamental
Castorbean	Ricinus communis	Severe diarrhea	Ornamental may escape

PLANT COMMON NAME	PLANT SCIENTIFIC NAME	SIGNS OF POISONING	HABITAT
Tobacco, tree tobacco	Nicotiana spp	Convulsions, then depression; sweating	Waste places
Chokecherry, wild cherry	Prunus virginiana	Difficult breathing, convulsions, rapid death, bright red blood	Stream sides

For more detailed information about poisonous plants you may wish to consult the *Field Guide to Plants Poisonous to Livestock - Western U. S.*, published by Rosebud Press, P.O. Box 270090, Fruitland, Utah 84027. This is an excellent reference with detailed information and line drawings. The author, Shirley Weathers, raises and packs with llamas.

Appendix Four:
BOOKS, VIDEOTAPES, MAGAZINES AND MAPS

Books about llamas

To order check your local bookstore or call Clay Press Inc., Publications toll-free at 1-877-CAMELID or 209-295-7818.

Barkman, Betty & Paul, *Image of a Well-Trained Llama.* 46 pages, many photos. Revised edition, by a pair who have trained everything from elephants to reptiles, with much llama experience. $20

Bodington, Helen, *Llama Training On Your Own.* 40 pages and illustrations. Step by step training manual with instructions for catching, easy haltering, desensitizing, loading and more. Special emphasis on training alone. $18.75

Burt, Sandi, *Llamas An Introduction to Care, Training and Handling,* 141 pages, photos, diagrams, charts. This book can help the first-time llama owner understand and enjoy llamas, and will be a handy reference for the experienced owner. $16.95

Harmon, David and Rubin, Amy S., *Llamas on the Trail - A Packer's Guide,* 170 pages with black and white photos and illustrations. Two experienced llama packers and writers thoroughly discuss llama packing. $15.00

Hart, Rosana, *Living With Llamas*, 192 pages with 60 photos. Heartwarming account of one couple's years with llamas, with practical information worked into the story. $14.95

Hoffman, Clare DVM and Asmus, Ingrid, *Caring for Llamas and Alpacas,* 171 pages, over 60 illustrations. Every llama owner should have this comprehensive guide to llama care. Excellent information for prospective, new and experienced owners. $23.95

Ingram, Gwen, *Evaluating a Llama Pack*, 27 pages. Step-by step explanations on proper procedures for fitting and using any llama pack. Clear line drawings and carefully presented text guide the reader through each of the many issues involved in a pack system evaluation. $5.95

Markham, Doyle, *Llamas are the Ultimate*, 330 pages, 73 photos. Training, feeding, packing, hunting, fishing and care. $14.95

McGee, Marty, with Linda Tellington-Jones, *Llama Handling and Training, the TTEAM Approach*. 224 pages with over 100 illustrations. Comprehensive manual on TTEAM methods for llamas, with case histories, photos, diagrams. $24.75

Videotapes about llamas

To order call Clay Press, Inc., Publications toll-free at 1-877-CAMELID or 209-295-7818.

All About Llamas video series with Paul and Sally Taylor. Tape #1 - *Llama Basics* 40 minutes. Comprehensive and entertaining introduction to the world of llamas. Tape #2 - *Breeding, Birthing and Newborn Care* 60 minutes with handbook. A practical guide to a successful breeding operation. Tape #3 - *Let's Go Packing* - Includes the basics of training, conditioning and equipment tips for packers. All tapes $40.00 each

Getting Started with TTEAM with Marty McGee. One hour video on basic TTEAM training techniques. $34.95

Treating Your Lama Kindly -Techniques for Veterinarians, Technicians and Owners with Dr. LaRue Johnson PhD and Marty McGee. Shows how to get the "job" done and still preserve and perhaps enhance a companionable relationship with llamas and alpacas. Just over two hours. $48.00

Llama Trekkers, by Paul and Betty Barkman. This video is a training experience for those ready to train their first packers. $39.95

Periodicals about llamas

Subscription rates as of January 1999 and subject to change - inquire when ordering.

The Backcountry Llama - edited by Noel McRae, 2857 Rose Valley Loop, Kelso, Washington 98626 *llamapacker@kalama.com.* An information-sharing newsletter published six times per year, dedicated to all aspects of packing with llamas. Equipment reviews, classified ads for pack llamas. $18 for five issues

The Link - P.O. Box 7907, Kalispell, Montana 59904. Monthly newsprint publication containing ads, information, event listings and a few articles. $12.00

Llamas Magazine - P.O. Box 250, Jackson, California 95642 *claypres@volcano.net.* Color magazine published five times per year filled with articles on llama health, training, auctions, personalities, upcoming events, and much more. Base Camp report regularly features packing-related articles. $20 per year.

Llama Life II - 5232 Blenheim Road, Charlottesville, Virginia 22902 Quarterly publication reporting llama and alpaca news and coming events. $20 per year.

Other books

Camp cooking

Latimer, Carole *Wilderness Cuisine*. Wilderness Press, 1991. Excellent recipes for gourmet wilderness dining.

McHugh, Gretchen, *The Hungry Hiker's Book of Good Cooking.* Alfred A. Knofp, 1982. A favorite camp cookbook.

Llama Rancher's Favorite Family Recipes - compiled by members of the International Llama Association, P.O. Box 1891, Kalispell, Montana 59903. $17.95 post paid. Features section of llama packer's recipes for trekking. Profits from sales go to support llama related programs nationwide.

Horse and mule packing

Back, Joe, *Horses, Hitches and Rocky Trails.* Johnson Books, Boulder, Colorado. A good book on traditional packing methods; lots of stories and illustrations.

Elser, Smoke and, Brown, Bill, *Packing in on Horses and Mules.* Mountain Press Publishing Company, Missoula, Montana, 1980. Lots of good photos and practical information on traditional hitches.

Livestock information

Haynes, N. Bruce D.V.M. *Keeping Livestock Healthy.* Garden Way Publishing, 1983. Basic information on livestock health concerns, including nutrition, diseases and treatments.

Plant field guides

Craighead, Creaghead and Davis, *A Field Guide to Rocky Mountain Wildflowers.* Houghton Mifflin Company, 1963. Excellent plant photos and descriptions.

James, Wilma Roberts, *Know your Poisonous Plants.* Naturegraph Publishers, 1973. Guide to plants poisonous to humans, with line drawings, descriptions of the plants and signs of poisoning.

Niehaus, Theodore F. and Ripper, Charles L., *A Field Guide to Pacific States Wildflowers*. Houghton Mifflin Company, 1976. Many drawings, minimal descriptions.

Weathers, Shirley A., *Field Guide to Plants Poisonous to Livestock - Western U.S.*, Rosebud Press, P.O. Box 270090, Fruitland, Utah 84027. Excellent reference with detailed information and line drawings. Author raises and packs with llamas.

USGS Topographical maps

You may refer to your local phone book's yellow pages for the nearest commercial dealers that sell USGS topographic maps and contact them directly for pricing and ordering information. For other information or ordering assistance, call 1-800-HELP-MAP, or write:

> USGS Information Services
> Box 25286
> Denver, Colorado 80225
> USGS Website: http://mapping.usgs.govt

Appendix Five:
LLAMA TRAINING CLINICIANS

Below is a list of several trainers who offer clinics that can help you train and work with your llamas. Many llama publications have a list of upcoming clinics in the "coming events" section, and for more information about individual trainers' offerings you may contact them directly. Some have books and videos available—consult the previous Appendix for listings.

Stanlynn Daugherty
Learn to Llama Pack Clinics
63366 Pine Tree Road
Enterprise, Oregon 97828
(541)432-4455
stanlynn@oregontrail.net / www.hcltrek.com

Charlie Hackbarth
Learn to Pack Clinics
Box 548
LaVeta, Colorado 81055
1-800-767-7479 / (719)742-5152
mslu@rmi.net

Jim Logan
Click & Reward Training
Rt. 3, Box 78
Chattaroy, Washington 99003-8507
1-888-332-5425 / (509)238-4975

Marty McGee
Cutting Edge Training for Llamas and Alpacas
403 Apodaca Hill
Santa Fe, New Mexico 87501
1-800 TTEAM-70 / (505)983-0775
martylama@aol.com

John Mallon
Mallon Method Clinics
19526 Rancho Ballena Road
Ramona, California 92065-5433
1-800-594-7254 / (760)789-7944
llamatrnr@aol.com / www.mallonmethod.com

Appendix Six:
LLAMA ORGANIZATIONS

Listed below are several national organizations for llama enthusiasts. Since all South American camelids-llamas, alpacas, guanacos and vicunas - are of the genus "lama," some associations use that all-encompassing word in their name.

ILA publishes a series of excellent educational brochures on llama care, a newsletter, and maintains a list of veterinarians that will consult with local vets on llama issues. Call 1-800-WHY-LAMA for a free "Llama Catalog" directory of llama products and services that includes contact information for 26 regional affiliated organizations and an extensive listing of publications and other print and video resources. The ILA Pack Committee works with various agencies to educate land managers and promote packing.

> International Llama Association
> P.O. Box 1891
> Kalispell, Montana 59903
> 1-800-WHY-LAMA
> e-mail: ILA@ InternationalLlama.org
> www.internationalllama.org

The ILR maintains an official genealogical registry and research system for llamas and other camelids.

> International Lama Registry
> P.O. Box 8
> Kalispell, Montana 59903
> (406)755-3438 / fax (406) 755-3439
> e-mail: ilr@digisys.net / www.lamaregistry.net

LANA publishes a quarterly newsletter, sponsors an annual Llama Expo, and has a national youth program.

Llama Association of North America
1800 S. Obenchaine Road
Eagle Point, Oregon 97524
541-826-6115
e-mail: llamainfo@aol.com

The Pack Llama Trial Association sanctions performance events across the country in an effort to preserve and promote the pack llama.

Pack Llama Trial Association
P.O. Box 25
Meridian, Idaho 83680-0025
e-mail: cclsheehan@sprintmail.com/
    www.netnow.micron.net/~llamahll/PLT/PLT.html

Appendix Seven:
SUPPLIERS OF LLAMA PACKS
AND OTHER EQUIPMENT

FLAMING STAR LLAMA PACK SYSTEMS, 11742 Highway 39, Klamath Falls, Oregon 97603 (541)882-8143 e-mail: Sidpacks@aol.com Top quality pack systems. *Recommended*

THE LLAMA CONNECTION, 8005 West Buckskin, Pocatello, Idaho 83201 (208)232-6456 or 1-800-398-0832. Saddles and other equipment as well as information on Classic 2000 llamas.

LLAMAS AND MORE STORE, 65260 Gerking Market Road, Bend, Oregon 97701 (541)317-1553, fax (541)317-1554 e-mail: llamasandmore@coinet.com / www.llamasandmore.com Complete catalog of gear for llama and miniature donkey owners.

MT. SOPRIS LLAMAS UNLTD., Box 548, LaVeta, Colorado 81055 1-800-767-7479 / (719)742-5152 e-mail: mslu@rmi.net All sorts of gear for packing, from halters to accurate load scales. Top-quality packs. Free catalog. *Recommended*

OLLIE LLAMAS, 2765 Hwy. 91 N., Dillon, Montana 59725 (406)683-2228 e-mail: olliellamas@mcn.net/www.olliellamas.com Pack systems, llama equipment, and more goodies. Free catalog.

ROCKY MOUNTAIN LLAMAS, 7202 N 45th St., Longmont, Colorado 80503 303-530-5575 phone or fax; e-mail: rkymtllama@aol.com/www.rockymtllamas.com Halters, packs and other equipment. Free catalog. *Recommended*

TIMBERLINE LLAMAS, INC., 30361 Rainbow Hills Road, Golden, Colorado 80401 303-526-0092. Pack saddle systems.

USEFUL LLAMA ITEMS, 3540 76th St., Caledonia, Michigan 49316 1-800-635-5262, fax (616)698-0870. e-mail: sales @useful-items.com/www.useful-items.com All manner of llama and ranch supplies. Free catalog.

ZEPHYR FARM, 4251 Pulver Road, Dundee, New York 14837 607-243-5282, fax 607-243-5866 Specializing in halters that fit, as well as TTEAM / Cutting Edge training books and videos.

Appendix Eight:
BASIC CHECKLIST FOR LLAMA BUYERS

No one, not even an expert, can pick out the perfect llama every time — for that matter, the "perfect llama" is only an ideal, not a living reality. However, some basic information and careful examination can greatly increase anyone's odds of acquiring a suitable llama. This sheet has been formulated to assist prospective buyers make their own evaluations and decisions, and is provided courtesy of the author, Gwen Ingram, and *The Backcountry Llama Newsletter.*

For any llama:

Preferred	Caution advised	Not recommended
Comfortable being approached in pen	Can be caught	Cannot catch in pen
Halters easily; halter is easily removed	Can halter and remove halter	Cannot safely halter, unhalter, or both
Leads easily	Llama will lead	Llama will not lead (evaluate several times to be sure nervousness is not the cause)
Front legs reasonably straight when viewed from front; walks freely without contacting opposite legs or feet	Slight deviation at front knees, walk not flowing	Very noticeable deviation at front knees; llama's legs or feet contact opposite legs or feet when walking normally
Males over 24 months: • castrated between 15 and 24 months — OR — • has two average-sized testicles present and a clearly stated reproductive guarantee Females: • spayed — OR — • normal external genitalia and clearly stated reproductive and use-specific guarantee	Males: • not castrated — OR — • normal testicles; no guarantees • castrated between 12 and15 months • castrated after 28 months Females: • not spayed — OR — • normal genitalia; no guarantees	Males: • one testicle • unusual testicular size (too large or too small) • castrated prior to 12 months Females: • visual genital irregularities • current or history of chronic uterine infection • spayed prior to 12 months
Can pick up all four feet	Llama allows upper legs to be touched and/or some feet to be picked up	Llama kicks or becomes violent when upper legs are touched
Males over 24-30 months: fighting teeth have been blunted or cut to 1/4" with dull surfaces		Males over 24-30 months: fighting teeth need blunting, cutting, or recutting.
Llama is groomed appropriately: • combed out if classic type • shorn and top-brushed if for wool use	Llama's wool type can be discerned, but has some mats and/or accumulated dead wool (puffy feeling) beneath surface	Llama is matted throughout
Llama is at an appropriate weight	Llama is moderately overweight	Llama is grossly obese or markedly thin

Compatible with most other llamas	Overly dependent on other llamas	Incompatible with most other llamas
Guarantee of satisfaction or suitability		

Additional steps for evaluating pack prospects:

Preferred	Caution advised	Not recommended
Personable, willing, enjoyable to be with	Withdrawn (may be frightened of strange surroundings) or unusually friendly	Jumpy or frightened of people; does not respect personal space (pushy or nosy)
Confident when alone with handler		Overly dependent on other llamas
Walks at an average (not rushed) hiking speed without dragging or slowing		Cannot or will not keep up with the average speed of the prospective buyer/hiker
Abundant guard hair, low wool density, short neck wool and no wool (hair only) on lower legs	Some guard hair with higher wool density; or unusually low wool density	Little or no guard hair; very dense fiber; long neck wool; lower leg wool
Can be touched on legs, belly, chest, back, and rump	Nervous about being touched	Will not tolerate contact or only tolerates contact in a few areas, such as the neck and withers
Back is free of sores, lumps, tenderness, scar tissue	White patches of hair on an otherwise dark llama; missing wool	Sore or tender spots, lumps or scars
Backline (feel) rises slightly and runs smoothly from withers to pelvis		Back is lower or noticably higher at the pelvis compared to the withers (when standing on level ground); back is sagging or swayed
Angle of hock and stifle joints noticeable; feet are placed under center of pelvis	Feet are placed behind pelvis when standing relaxed	Angle of hock and stifle joints almost straight; greater-than-normal angle at hock and stifle joints; feet consistantly placed in front of pelvis
No deviation or extremely slight deviation at knee joint when viewed from front		Noticeable deviation at knee joint
Front legs are straight when viewed from side		Knees "bow out" to the front or "cave in" toward the rear

Pasterns form an angle of approximately 75° with the ground when standing; angle of 60° at maxium flexxion		Soft pasterns (sink noticeably with each stride); low pastern angle; fetlocks touch the ground when walking; llama under four years of age and one or both parents have soft pasterns; pasterns appear upright
Toes generally face forward when walking; travels on two narrow tracks	Feet (fore, hind, or both) track very close to a single line	Toes pointed very much out or in; feet track on a single line or cross over during stride
Total body length appears about the same as the distance from the llama's back to the ground when the llama is standing normally		Body is definitely longer than the llama's height at the withers
From side, llama moves flowingly and relaxed with the neck held relaxed and forward; visible topline moves regularly and with minimal up-and-down motion at the pelvis; large, long strides	Neck held higher than normal (may be nervousness); pelvis bobs up and down	Jerky or abrupt movements; neck held nearly straight out, or straight up and stiff; small strides; limping
From front, llama moves evenly and balanced		Llama moves with definite side-to-side motion or waddle, and/or appears to have a wide chest
From rear, llama moves evenly and balanced and with firmness	Llama's rear end seems to teeter or wobble slightly when moving slowly	Llama moves with side-to-side motion or waddle; rear end teeters, wobbles, or jerks
Guarantee of suitability/performance with refund or suitable exchange; verbal or pictorial evidence of trail experience and/or parental & sibling performance		No guarantees or performance history in llama or immediate relations; llama used for packing heavy loads prior to physical maturity

INDEX

A

Abscesses 47
Activated charcoal 188
Alarm call 58–59
Andes 4

B

Bachelor herd 57, 60
Balking 92, 114, 141–142
Banamine 187, 192, 195
Banjo (llama) 81, 158
Barns 53
Bears 162, 165
Bells 80
"Berserk male syndrome" 27
Betadine 186, 187, 190, 196
Books about llamas 235
Bottle-fed llamas 27
Britchin' 69, 73
Build of llamas 21–22
Bureau of Land Management
    (BLM) 125, 204
Butazolidin 187, 192

C

Calmness of llamas 5, 138
Carmilax 188, 195
Catch pen 56, 86
Catching llamas 86–87
Checklist for llama buyers 244
Chest
    desirable width 22
Children and llamas 6
Cinches 69
    placement of 73, 106
    training to accept 103–104, 105
Clostridial diseases, vaccination
    against 47

Commercial llama packing 199–
    211
Conditioning
    evaluating on llama 24–25, 50
    in preparation for packing
        113, 143
Conformation 21–22, 245, 246
Connector, rubber band 213
Cookboxes 179
Coolers 177–179
Costs of llamas 5, 11, 30, 36, 41
Coyote (llama) 79, 159, 190
Crowding (tail-gaiting) on the trail
    139–140
Crupper 69, 73
Cupcake (llama) 20, 40, 46, 61–
    62, 66, 157, 211

D

Donkeys 9, 10
Downhill hiking 139
Dung piles 53, 66, 155, 160, 168
Dust wallow 54, 165, 168

E

Ectrin 196
Electrolyte replacer
    45, 186, 188, 193
Environment
    impact of llamas on 10
    minimizing effect on
        137, 156, 166–167, 183
Equipment for packing 76–
    78, 166
    list 77
    suppliers 243

247

Llamas
Magazine

Sub Card

$20 For One Year - 5 Issues! (Includes Special Herd Sire Edition)
Canadian orders add $5; International add $10
❏ **Bill me - or call (209) 295-7800 to order**

Name _____

Address _____

City/State/Zip _____

Name _____

Address _____

City _____ State _____ Zip _____

Telephone (____) _____

P.O. Box 250
Jackson, CA 95642
Toll Free: 1-(877)-CAMELID

CLAY PRESS, INC. Publications

Quantity	Order Number	Book Title	Price	Unit Price	Total

MasterCard/Visa/Discover
Acct. # _____
Expiration Date _____
Phone (____) _____
Signature _____

Shipping/Handling - U.S.A./Canada
Up to $25.00/$5.00,
$25.01 to $50.00/$6.75,
$50.01 to $75.00/$8.00,
$75.01 to $100.00/$9.00,
$100.01 to $125.00/$9.75,
$125.01 to $150.00/$10.50,
$150.01 Over/$11.25.

Sub Total	
7.25% CA Tax	
Ship/Handle	
Total Enclosed	$